WALK ON THE GRASS

www.angelawhitlock.com

Links

In the electronic edition of this manual, words in blue type are linked to URLs on the World Wide Web,

e.g. www.walk-on-the-grass.com

Chapter titles in the Table of Contents are linked to their respective chapters. Left clicking with your mouse will take you to the associated destination. URLs require an active internet connection.

Disclaimer

License Agreement

Copyright Information

All Rights Reserved.

Whitlock-Boyle Ltd registered in England No. 6688310.

Registered Office Address: C/O SJD Accountancy

1200 Century Way, Thorpe Park Business Park, Colton, Leeds LS15 8ZA

Website URL: www.angelawhitlock.com
Email: info@angelawhitlock.com
www.Walk-On-The-Grass.com

ISBN 978-0-9565024-0-7

Printed March 2010

WALK ON THE GRASS

Angela Whitlock

D.Hyp, PGD.Hyp, BSCH(Mem), Cert Ed.

Edited by Anthony Skidmore

TABLE OF CONTENTS

Acknowledgements

I have met many people who have re-written their own rule books and inspired me but none so great an influence as my oldest brother, who despite the most difficult of health and every imaginable obstacle, he has overcome many challenges, whilst remaining the most forward thinking, inspirational person I know.

I dedicate this book to you, James Boyle and thank you for all the early influence you knitted into my character that has encouraged me to believe in myself for many years. You give back to people so much more than you take and with a humility that is rare in any human being. Together we are a third of a large wonderful family who benefitted from having two great parents throughout our lives, Thomas and Martha Boyle.

I would also like to thank my partner Andy and all my family, Richard, Christine, Hazel and Fiona who have assisted with so many aspects of the book including a great deal of laughter along the way. And a special thank you to my friends, particularly Joey Parkin for all her invaluable graphical input.

Finally a huge thank you to Anthony Skidmore and Pete Fulham. Tony who edited the book and kicked my ramblings into shape, you are better than a personal trainer, and Pete Fulham who helped with the technical knowhow.

Preface

Walk on the Grass is a book aimed at inspiring those of you who are ready to ignore what keeps you from moving on, and rooted to the past, into a world full of greater success and personal achievement. Step by step, it seeks to help you break the old habits and ways of thinking that prevent you from taking positive action to improve every aspect of your life. It has been designed as a kick-start to reboot your creative and emotional capability into gear, and ensure it continues working at the highest level.

All too often it is the little things that worry us and restrict us from taking real action. This book will start you on that journey, into a more creative, productive lifestyle, where balance means so much more than something you see on your bank statement. But first, let me share with you a short story that happened to me and made me realise how sometimes even the most simplest of decisions in life are often the most difficult. Walk on the Grass will share with you ideas to make those small decisions so much easier to make because many times the only person making the rules is you, and if you made them you can change them so get ready to break down some of those walls you've built up that form the rule book of your life.

Imagine the scene: A mature, responsible and very well paid Project Manager was pacing the floor. He had a decision to make and was totally unsure with regard to the outcome. The fear he was feeling was visible in his whole body language as the anxiety within him gradually escalated, causing psychological as well as physiological stress. With a dark expression, he pondered the consequences of the decision he was about to make. The outside observer could be forgiven for wondering at the magnitude of that decision. Was it a life and death situation? Were millions of pounds of company money at stake? Well, fortunately not. It was simply that Brian, like a great many of us from time to time, was unnecessarily deliberating on a matter that could have been resolved very easily. The question that was pressing like a great weight down on his shoulders was this: Could he leave the office early because his mother needed his assistance?

One can only guess at his inner thinking: Would the wheels of industry grind to a halt if he left the office early? Would his staff be lost and helpless without him? Would the entire office go into meltdown in his absence? The answer, of course, had Brian been able to consider it reasonably, was that none of things were likely to happen just because he had a real and genuine need to leave the office slightly earlier than usual.

The real stress, however, was caused because Brian could not decide on the options that were open to him in resolving his dilemma. As far as he could understand it they were as follows: A) Should he ask his own boss for permission to leave early, even though this person wasn't in the office at the time, and thereby risk the wrath of someone he perceived as difficult or: B) Simply inform his team of his intentions and leave. It may seem such a simple decision that many of us would give no time at all to, but on that day it was important to Brian. His own rule book told him so.

After observing my colleague struggle with his dilemma, I finally walked up to him and said, as good-humouredly as possible: "Sometimes Brian, you just have to walk on the grass". He laughed, clearly understanding the meaning of the metaphor. It really was a simple decision and not one worthy of stress and the remark appeared to rationalise his thinking immediately, giving him permission to end his frustrating inner stalemate and unnecessary self-imposed rules. "If the boss turns up, just tell her I left early because I had to sort something out," he said, grinning a little sheepishly as he moved towards the door. One chance remark and his rule book had been altered because sometimes we just need to be aware that we have to break some of our own rules to walk on the grass.

So feet at the ready and feel that luxurious soft green grass underfoot.................

Introduction

WELCOME TO WALK ON THE GRASS

Walk on the Grass is not a theoretical text book intent on giving the meaning and method of creativity. Books stores and libraries are already awash with books discussing the life and works of Leonardo Di Vinci and the genius of Albert Einstein. This book is plainly and simply a desire to share with you simple techniques learned after 30 years of study and experience, on how to awaken your own creativity and challenge your emotional thinking to set aside the limiting self-imposed rules you may have inadvertently created for yourself.

Creativity is so much more than playing a musical instrument, writing or painting a picture. Creativity can aid and influence every decision you make. The development and use of your own creativity is essential for your own future growth, and for that of the world in which you live.

Children don't have rules; the grass is a carpet of fun to them!

I always find it surprising therefore, that so many of us find it so difficult to demonstrate or even admit to the existence of our creative side. And why is that so much of our **creativity tends to diminish** as we ourselves grow older?

Indirectly we are **programmed** both at home and school to toe the line, to conform and to be wary of signs of creativity that could make us more exciting as people, or outside of the norm of things. Instead we have to wait for suitable instructions, to be given permission before we can begin to find that lost creativity again. By developing your creative awareness, you will give yourself the permission to have fun, to enjoy the company of those around you and to really feel what life is about.

There is sufficient evidence to demonstrate that children at three or four years old are **entirely free** of any social or self restraints, and can therefore be witnessed literally walking on the grass at every opportunity.

The sign that says 'don't' is of little consequence to them. The grass is a playground, a **green luxurious carpet**, a soft landing place, a running track In fact; it is anything their imaginations can make of it. But it is never 'a no go area!'

It is however, unfortunately, shortly after this age, that their parents, teachers or guardians; in fact anyone and everyone who claims to have their very best interests at heart, will slowly, or sometimes even frantically, begin introducing the sobering rules of society to these once **uninhibited minds**.

By the age of 10, children are already becoming more aware of the 'rules of freedom' and, in corresponding measure, their creativity now begins diminishing. The toy that was once their best friend in the world has now become only an acquaintance. They are told how to be creative rather than just allowing their imagination to flourish. For example at school they follow instructions on what to draw rather than have the freedom to be inspired by their own thoughts.

By the age of 13, children become more self-conscious, concerned at evoking criticism when writing, painting, and singing in public, or dancing in the kitchen, as they once did completely uninhibited and without the slightest feeling of self-consciousness. Their once adorable creativity toy is now being left high and unreachable on the shelf, only to be taken down on the rarest of occasions.

At 16, children are now so 'cool' and self conscious that any spontaneous act is a very rare event indeed, something that is likely to occur only in safe surroundings and with a few very trusted and close friends to view the spectacle. The attraction of the creativity toy is now also fading fast, becoming something of a sickly and embarrassing friend, who is no longer fun to play with. Having now lost its sparkle, it is put away with the other old toys, boxed up in the attic along with other youthful belongings that are no longer required.

By the age of 25, creativity can be all but non-existent. Seriousness, responsibility and the realities of life have smothered it. There is no longer time for fun, for spontaneity. There is virtually no time for creativity at all.

If you still doubt the suspicion with which adults view their creative possibilities, I would suggest you tell the next stranger you meet that you are an artist. And then see how quickly the stranger points out to you that they 'can't paint or 'can't draw'. When they tell you this ask them why, did they forget how to. That is, the ones who are bold enough to reply. This is because our creativity has been moulded out of us, in very subtle influential ways.

This is a journey to **reclaim** that sense o**f freedom and inspired thinking** that, for so many, disappeared when that creative toy was boxed up in the attic. So stay with me, and together, let's re-energise those creative brainwaves that will undoubtedly lead you to greater personal success and fulfilment.

The fact is that when you are creative, you are also enthusiastic and full of motivation. Creativity also inspires fresh and new ideas, and innovative new ways of thinking and acting.
Creativity nurtures the mind as nature nurtures the soil, planting seeds which:

* **Inspire** improvement in so many other aspects of your life, usually where you would least expect it to.
* Trigger **original** ideas and entirely new ways of thinking.
* Allow those wonderful **'light bulb'** moments when you realise that solutions can be so simple and obvious
* Shed **light** in the darkness. When your world may seem to be in crisis, creativity gives us the ability to find direction when we most need it.

SOME IDEAS TO GET YOU STARTED

The format of this book is very simple. In order to follow the various exercises and techniques, all you will require is a **small note book**, preferably one that will fit neatly into a pocket or handbag. You can also use this portable notebook as your own personal diary or journal, charting ideas and moments of inspiration, as well as providing a commentary of your progress.

A client of mine once informed me that he always felt more positive and achieved a greater level of success, if he wrote down on paper a list of **daily tasks** he wanted to complete. He told me that it made him feel more secure, and it also seemed to take the pressure away from him. Ticking off each task as it was successfully completed also gave him a great sense of confidence and achievement.

POETRY IN MOTION

Everyone has negative thoughts from time to time, but it's where you channel those thoughts that really matters. One way of relieving those dull thoughts or ideas, when they begin to loop repetitively through your mind, causing you to feel low, disheartened and anxious, is to record your thoughts and feelings by simply writing them down. In this way your thoughts become crystallised, and are transformed from intangibles into something more solid, making them easier to deal with.

You can do this creatively in the form of a **poem or limerick**. Capturing unhelpful thoughts in this way can often also ignite new ideas, and in turn induce a feeling of calm and relaxation. The result of this is that your mood will inevitably lift, because it is psychologically impossible to feel relaxed and anxious at the same time. You don't need to be the next poet laureate when putting your thoughts into words, but simply express yourself honestly, using your own personal vocabulary. I offer my own example of the thoughts that were passing through my mind, in a poem I wrote while waiting for a train on a very cold winter's day;

THE RAT TRAIN

Waiting, queuing, when is it here?
Am I in the right place, will it stop near?
Shuffle a bit; nudge along, near to the door
I better get a seat, a nice group of four

Standing tiresome in the pouring rain
Will it be on time, or late, what a pain?
Day in, day out, let the race commence
Shoulders held tight so rigid so tense

Anticipation hanging in the morning air
Stand to attention but not over there
Movement already in the race today
Who caused that sensation, no train yet we say

Oh it's arriving, excitement, get a place
Shift right, shift left, get the door at your face
Converging into one, who gets on first?
"I was before him", as we mumble and curse

At last on the train, in a comfortable seat
Shoulders relax, all quiet in the warmth and the heat
Move up, move down, and move over there
Herded and shuffled in one centimetre square

Arrive at the station, we prepare to alight
To repeat it again, tomorrow morning and night!

Recording your negative thoughts in a poem allows your mind to process and file them away, clearing the way for more positive, rewarding and imaginative thinking. Your journal will be invaluable and I would love to see your best poetry so feel free to send it to me at info@angelawhitlock.com.

RIGHT BRAIN THINKING

If, as you write, it seems that your mind is becoming tired, your imagination is drying up, and inspiration is leaving you altogether, try holding your **pen** in the **opposite hand.** You may not be able to write so clearly with your non-dominant hand, but you can make simple notes or just allow your pen to doodle or begin drawing creatively. Using the hand you usually don't use for writing can have an amazing effect in **triggering right brain** thinking, which is generally the part of the mind responsible for the creative aspects of your intelligence.

There is nothing that activates the mind more vigorously than a difficult challenge.

THE FIRST RULE YOU CAN BREAK

Now I know this is going to be a difficult challenge for you but it is important that you start breaking a few self-imposed rules early on in this journey. You now have my permission as the author, to write in this book; by any ways or means you choose to. Many of the activities are downloadable from my site at www.angelawhitlock.com but don't take the safe option; how liberated will you feel to do something that you were never allowed to do as a child? So off you go, write your name at the front and feel the freedom it generates, after all it's your book!

Chapter 1

Back to the Future

RE-ENGAGING WITH CHILDHOOD ACTIVITIES

"Don't let the Goats get in the canoe" said the Farmer. "Of course we won't" said the children. But a light went on in their imagination, as they walked away: "What a fantastic idea, do you think we could?" They whispered conspiratorially to each other.

Creative thinking in children is infectious, infiltrating into every corner of their life. And once it gathers momentum, it becomes like an eternal spring, which just keeps flowing and flowing. It is the most important facility for any area of human development. And the fact is that we are all born with an **unlimited creative potential**. We see it so clearly in children, who, without any conscious reasoning, play freely, paint, draw, dance and sing. In fact they express themselves in a thousand different ways, even encouraging goats to embark from dry land into a canoe.

When was the last time you played, painted, drew pictures, danced and sang – all in a single day? Creativity, you see, is not rationed, neither does it ever disappear. We don't just wake up one day and find we've lost it; it's simply that for some inexplicable reason we tend to use this **amazing facility** less and less as the years go by and we grow into adulthood.

So what is it that blocks our creativity? What stops it from flowing? Well, it's reasoned that one of the main inhibitors of creativity is **'responsibility'**. As we grow older, we begin to take responsibility for a great many factors involving our supposed well-being and sense of security. These can relate to our close relationships with our families, the upbringing of our children, as well as all the complex practical and financial matters related to simply keeping a roof over our head.

We become responsible for acquiring and keeping jobs, running cars, and, of course, paying the inevitable bills when they become due. The problem is that all this 'responsibility' keeps our conscious minds so preoccupied that we begin denying ourselves access to the unconscious mind, from which all creativity begins and flows. As a result the sheer weight of this 'responsibility' begins to drain us of inspiration, sapping our creativity in the way that a leech draws out the blood from its hosts.

But the truth is that it doesn't have to be like that. Your creative power is always there available to you, simply waiting for the **blue touch paper** to be lit once more to fire it into action.

The intention of this chapter is to light that blue touch paper. But in order to do that, we must first take you on a journey. And the journey will include a visit back to that wonderful state of carefree childhood creativity you experienced before responsibility took over and suppressed it. But it's not simply a journey down memory lane. This section of the book will show you how to reunite with your own **childhood creativity**, and how to bring it back with you into your new future. Because it really is time now for your creativity to fully wake up, and begin moving you towards achieving the personal success you so richly deserve.

So, what route must we take in order to begin being more creative? Before we can answer this question, it's necessary to discover what creativity actually means to you. Perhaps you might like to jot down what you already remember of some of those **creative activities** in your note book or journal now, before you carry out the following exercise:

❀ I'm creative when.....................................
❀ I'm inspired when ....
❀ I'm relaxed when ....
❀ I'm imaginative when...................................
❀ The person that inspires me most is ....

You see, creativity can be interpreted in many different ways. Often it may be influenced by what you read in books, magazines or newspapers, or by what you see and hear on the television or radio. Your understanding of its meaning may also have been partially directed by the opinions of others. However, all this is now of no consequence. It's time for you to **make up your own mind**, and discover what creativity really means to you.

The object of this book, after all, is to inspire you to gain **greater personal success** and sufficient confidence to allow you to break your own rules in order to walk on the grass – just as children do naturally, without any fear of the consequences. And without doubt, the greatest tool to help you to achieve this is your own innate creativity.

A NATURAL ABILITY

Adapting my own experience in order to consider creativity as a child, leads me to define it as a **natural ability** incorporating the following criteria:

❀ Imagination

🌼 Innovation
🌼 Originality
🌼 Drive to Discover Solutions

IMAGINATION

One of the chief characteristics of creativity is the **imagination**. It is usually the starting point for all creativity:

🌼 Imagine if I could paint a picture
🌼 Imagine if I could run a business
🌼 Imagine if I could sing

INNOVATION

Taking **risks** and challenging rules is a central part of innovation. Yes, it's back to fearlessly walking on the grass, just as children do naturally as a matter of course.

To be really innovative is to do something no-one else has done before, or to go to places others have never been. Faced with baffling new technology, children will just **naturally** work out how to use it because they have no preconceived ideas, are unaware of the concept of failure, and *don't know how not to* resolve a problem.

ORIGINALITY OR INVENTIVENESS

Being **original** is the pinnacle of creativity, but it also involves making associations with other processes.

Children can be especially inventive in **linking** together items that haven't been associated before.

DRIVE TO DISCOVER SOLUTIONS

There's always an end result when creativity is applied. It may be a product, such as a completed painting or drawing, or a crafted object. But the completion of any project or object also means that you have discovered the **solution** to the problem of achieving the aim of that project or the completion of that object. It therefore follows that any act of creation involves a drive to discover a solution, creative people love looking for solutions.

32 THINGS TO DO BEFORE 11 YEARS OLD

In order to help you regain the path to your full creative potential, so that you can begin weaving it back into the fabric of your life, let's begin by looking at some typical creative **childhood activities**.

It's likely that in examining some of the **32 activities** appearing in the following list, you may be transported back in time, regardless of the march of new technology. It is, however, simply a list of 32 activities that most children may have experienced before reaching the age of eleven.

Now consider the following list and identify which activities you experienced as a child. It may be useful to make a note of each one in your journal or notebook, recalling your feelings at the time when you were experiencing the particular activity. And if **memories** you haven't had for a very long time suddenly come flooding back, don't be too surprised.

✱ Simply **put a tick** beside the activities you've actually experienced yourself as a child. If there are any you've never experienced, start thinking of ways you can do them now. The aim is for you to complete the entire list.

	32 things to do Before You Are 11 Years Old	✔
1	Bake cakes or buns	
2	Be in the middle of nowhere	
3	Build a damn	
4	Build a sand castle	
5	Camp out in the garden	
6	Chalk out a Hopscotch frame on your garden path and play it	
7	Climb a tree	
8	Collect frogspawn	
9	Come first in anything	
10	Do a handstand	
11	Dress up and wear heels	
12	Eat ice cream too fast and get brain freeze	
13	Hang upside down from a tree	
14	Have a snowball fight	
15	Have a water fight	
16	Jump a stream	
17	Make a boat out of leaves and twigs and get it to float	
18	Make a den in the garden	
19	Make a mud pie – or a sand pie	
20	Make a painting using your feet or hands	
21	Make snow angels	
22	Make something out of a cardboard box	
23	Outwit your mum or teacher	
24	Play pooh sticks	
25	Ride a bike	
26	See your favourite animal	
27	Sing on a karaoke	
28	Spin on a roundabout until you're dizzy	
29	Stand up for yourself	
30	Stay up all night	
31	Wake some worms up by stamping on the grass	
32	Watch fireworks	

When you recall each activity, or even when you **imagine** undertaking an activity, record your positive feelings about it. Was it fun? Was it enjoyable? How did you **feel** during the activity? Set your thoughts down clearly in your journal or notebook. By also using poems, pictures and **drawings**, you will be able to express your feelings more vividly. Make any illustrations as **bright** and **colourful** as possible. Recording notes and keeping photographs or drawings, which you can bring out whenever you want to, is a great visual way to reflect back on your experiences in the future, and of **lifting your mood** on a day when you may not be feeling on top of the world. There's nothing like a positive memory to bring you right back into balance.

Looking at things differently

However, if you regard this activity as time-wasting nonsense then it is quite probable that your creativity is really being stifled. After all, what you are doing is simply tapping into a **rich vein** of creativity, which may have been lying dormant since childhood. Once you actually give it a try, you may already feel it beginning to flow strongly again?

The care and welfare of children is, of course, a major responsibility which, at times, can cause great anxiety to parents. But recognising the creativity in a child, and sharing their **creative experiences** can, not only be a source of the greatest pleasure, but can forge a loving bond that will stay with you for all your life. Sharing creativity with your children invariably promotes deeper understanding, and allows the inevitable rifts and problems we all experience to fade far away into the background. It is also a way of converting the duty of child minding into a **positive pleasure**.

In making the effort to **re-engage** with your own children, grandchildren or nephews and nieces, by simply allowing yourself to play creatively, you will also be relieving yourself of the great weight we all carry inside that heavy rucksack of responsibility for a while. And you know how good it feels when you can finally put down a heavy load you've been carrying around too long. So begin to make that **connection** now by considering each of the 32 activities. Once your imagination gets into full flow, you may come up with many more creative ideas to link you back to childhood. I recommend that you are as innovative as possible.

To start the ball rolling, here's one example of creative play founded in childhood, and a particular favourite of mine. **'Snow Angels'** can be easily adapted when you go to bed at night. It is very simple:

- If you share your bed, ensure that you get into it a minute or two before your partner, or your activity could be entirely misconstrued!
- Centre yourself in your bed
- Wave your arms and legs as if you were doing a star jump, laid down.

Apart from the **playfulness** of this activity, and the physical exercise involved, the bed will get incredibly warm very quickly. It is likely that your partner will appreciate this - especially in winter. When you do things differently you open up new neural pathways in the brain that triggers new ways of thinking in all aspects of your life.

THE HUMBLE CARDBOARD BOX

Until he was thirteen years old, my son had a strange fascination for any new cardboard box that crossed our threshold. He was never very interested in the actual contents of the box, usually some labour-saving gadget that didn't fulfil its purpose at all. What really interested him and held his attention, were the possibilities of what he could create out of the box. Generally he favoured larger boxes. He would often use these to create a 'hide', concealing himself until some poor unsuspecting family member happened to pass by the box. Then, assuming his new identity as 'cardboard robot boy', he would suddenly leap up and frighten the life out of the innocent passer by. Usually it was me. The crudely cut out eyes should have been a giveaway, but those of you with children or child relatives will probably understand the attraction of **cardboard boxes**. Most of us will have had the experience of watching a child excitedly open an expensive present, and then within minutes discard the present in order to give their attention more fully to the container it came in.

Often parents despair at their failure to fascinate children with the latest, and usually most expensive, toy of the year. Unfortunately for them, however, children seldom concern themselves regarding the cost of a present; neither do they usually consider the difficulty you may have had in procuring it. Have you ever wondered why the present you were so sure would **delight** them, so often does not achieve the desired effect? Or is it, as many people may genuinely believe, that the child's reaction is simply:

a) To annoy the parents?

b) Because the present is boring?

c) Because they waited too long to receive it, and have now lost all interest in the process?

A child's ungracious and unenthusiastic reaction, of course, might be due to any of the above reasons. But more probably it is because within a few seconds of **playing** with the toy, the child has worked out exactly what it does and how it operates. The child has learned, for instance, that if you press a particular button or lever, or move this or that object, then the toy moves, walks, talks, makes a noise or performs some mechanical operation. In short, they learn how the toy functions more or less immediately.

Naturally curious, the child then looks around for some other distraction, something more interesting on which to re-focus their attention. It's usually at this stage that the pet cat or dog runs for the hills. 'So', the child may be thinking, 'what else is there still to **investigate**'? The curiosity of children knows no bounds. It is, after all, how they learn. And it is at this point that the child's attention is usually drawn to the box or even the wrapping paper in which the present arrived.

The child's imagination is then fired immediately, as he or she wonders exactly what this new object is? What does it do? What is it for? It's a conundrum the child feels duty-bound to **solve**. Is it a hat? They put the object on their head, deciding when they can't see anything, that perhaps it's too big for a hat. Then the thought may occur: "What will happen if I climb inside?" They child climbs inside and begins **laughing** perhaps, simply because it feels funny or pleasantly disorientating to be inside the box. Do you begin to understand what is going through the child's mind now? The child is not snubbing your expensive present or being ungrateful, it is simply investigating the **creative possibilities** of the box or the wrapping. In the child's lively imagination, the box could represent any number of wondrous possibilities, including:

✿	Car	✿	Doll house
✿	Train	✿	Police car
✿	Puppet Theatre	✿	Dog bed
✿	Castle	✿	Ambulance
✿	Fire truck	✿	Cave

The extent of a child's imagination should never be underestimated and we can learn so much from it. In the wonderful world of childhood everything becomes absorbing and interesting. It's how a child develops intelligence. So don't be disappointed or upset because you feel that your present has been rejected, but rather be joyful and amazed at the unlimited creativity of children.

Perhaps the next time you see a child discard the gift in favour of the packaging, you might try **nurturing** that creativity; attempt to discover what it is the child is trying to build, shape or imagine. And don't be surprised if you find your own imagination firing up as you allow yourself to become **pleasantly drawn** into the world of childhood creativity.

There are, of course, a great many lessons we can learn ourselves by studying our children more closely. Do we, for example, really need to start from the single premise of a blank piece of paper when we are seeking a **creative pathway** to solutions or ideas for change? Associating two or more unrelated items can be the trigger for sparking ideas that might otherwise never have come to mind.

A perfect example of simple **association** is the Post It Note. Used in most working environments now, Post It Notes, which came about through pure accident, combine an association of two products:

- Glue that didn't stick very well and
- Paper.

Who would have believed that something so simple that came about accidentally, or rather as a failure because the glue was too weak for its original purpose, would become a worldwide international product?

WHAT'S IN THE GARDEN SHED

In reviewing this chapter, our focus has been to **dig up** some old **childhood creativity**, and to establish your own **beliefs about creativity.** We have also suggested ways in which you can re-engage and inspire your own activity, by remembering and immersing yourself in the creative experiences of your own childhood.

- Enjoy the top **32 things to do before you are eleven** and get reacquainted with the fun you can have.
- The next time you're confronted by a **discarded cardboard box,** perhaps you too can consider the creative possibilities of making something out of what seems like nothing at all. The more you attempt to see the world through your children's eyes, the more you'll learn to engage with them and realise the joy that can come out of simple creative activity. There's no Blue Peter Badge in it for you, I'm afraid. But I do guarantee that that once you have

completed this chapter, you will begin to **understand** children much more and appreciate what it is they are attempting to do. But more than that, you will be starting to get back in touch with your own creativity. Restoring your **childhood creativity** may prove to be one of the most satisfying accomplishments possible, inspiring you to achieve so much more personal success in the future.

Remember ... childhood creativity never has to leave you again... so enjoy this first part of our journey, a journey to re-engage with your creativity and you'll develop this even further as we continue .... and we'll put this very effective tool to good use in the chapters still to come.

WALK ON THE GRASS

Chapter 2

One Person's Risk is Another Person's Reality

MAKING DECISIONS WORK FOR YOU

The financial adviser had come determined to sell a life insurance policy. He knew his business, and understood that his most effective selling ploy was based on instigating the fear of the unknown. Using all his guile, he paused, turning to the woman's partner, before delivering what he hoped would be the killer question: "Andy, what do you think Angela would do if you died?" Andy paused thoughtfully for a moment before answering: "I imagine she'd get a lodger in", he finally replied. The salesman was stunned. It wasn't the answer he'd been hoping for or expecting. Unfortunately for him he had underestimated this couples' attitude to risk and reality

During Patricia's late teens, she was particularly competitive with the younger of her brothers. He was in fact just three years older than her. As with most siblings, she observed with interest, fascination and, not least, more than a little frustration, how he would constantly ignore fabulous opportunities whenever they arose. His reaction was always the same when confronted with these opportunities; he simply considered only what could go wrong, and seldom what was likely to go well. In short, he allowed himself to become a victim of his fears.

Of course, he was **incredibly creative** with his excuses for not taking these wonderful opportunities. The excuses were always ready and they were numerous. Often it was: "You don't understand Pat, you don't have responsibilities, like I do". And later, when she could indeed claim to have her own share of genuine 'responsibilities', the excuses became less creative, and more succinct. In fact they were reduced to a rather feeble: "You don't understand ".

The point was that Patricia understood completely. She knew that the difference between them could be summed up as follows: what her brother considered as a **risk,** she deemed to be a **reality.**

Fear is an all consuming emotion that can literally stop us in our tracks. It is possibly the most destructive of all the emotions. It can paralyse our thoughts and actions. Confronted by fear, we literally stand still. But we are only born with two basic fears; all others are gathered along the way. Those innate fears are:

* Fear of loud noises
* Fear of falling

In order for you to walk on the grass in your own life, free, **liberated** and with **positive** faith in the future, fear must be addressed as soon as it appears.

Perhaps unsurprisingly, a recent scientifically-based report claims that 7 out of 10 people suffer from a specific fear or phobia. Many of these fears can be linked to **conditioned responses** to animals or inanimate objects, and are well documented. But perhaps a much more common fear is the fear of **change** itself. This is the very real fear, sometimes close to dread, that you may experience when you consider changing jobs or careers, even though that change is likely to vastly improve the quality and sense of fulfilment of your life.

> *What do you fear most at the moment?*
> *Make a list of all the fears you have that you can think of?*
> *Which do you have sole control of?*

You can only change the things over which you have control. But sometimes even though you feel you have no control, you may well have more than you realise.

During the interviews I've held with so many people over the years, I've listened to the recurring theme of what it is these people wish to move away from. They can tell me quite clearly and succinctly. There is no hesitation in doing so. And yet no matter how great the desire for change may be, so often the actual fear of moving towards something **different** proves to be even more dreaded than a continuation of the life they yearn to change.

It is therefore important that you learn to fully understand the **nature** and consequences of change. In order to do this, we also need to consider the fear factor that so often accompanies those changes. It is a universal truth that everyone, at one time or another, experiences fear. What is less understood is the way in which fear can actually **fire our creativity** and easily transform itself into excitement. This is because the mind can't actually differentiate between the two very differing emotions. The 'flight or fight principle' is always evoked when we are experiencing extremes of emotion. Whether it's **positive excitement** or negative fear, the mind and body are put in a heightened state of preparation, in which the same physiological and psychological sensations are experienced.

Consider these common reactions to the presence of fear:

Symptom
• **You can think of nothing else, but what is going to take place or what has happened**
• **You heart skips a beat and you get palpitations**
• **Your blood pressure rises and your skin flushes**
• **Your throat dries up and saliva reduces**
• **You might tremble**

Did you notice that the same reactions are present when confronted by both fear and excitement, and trigger the same responses in both the mind and body? The truth is that fear and excitement are therefore separated by just a few neurons, by the smallest amount of electro-chemical signalling. Learning to **relax the mind** is by far the greatest way of releasing unnecessary fear, and we will examine effective ways in which to instigate a calm relaxed mind in later chapters.

POWERFUL DECISION MAKING

Your subconscious is one of the most **powerful** under-utilised facilities you possess. And it's yours, uniquely yours, a remarkable power-house of information of potential. In order to appreciate its tremendous possibilities, let's begin by examining just one of its many facilities, its enormous **storage capacity**.

It is estimated that the subconscious part of your mind has been carefully and accurately filing and storing away information for 5,256,000 minutes for every decade you have lived. You see now why teenagers think they know so much!

To put this into context, consider the following calculations, based over four decades of life:

- 🌱 **20 years old** : 10,512,000 minutes of information stored
- 🌱 **30 years old**: 15,768,000 minutes of information stored
- 🌱 **40 years old**:   21,024,000 minutes of information stored

It's estimated that more or less a third of this time is spent in sleeping. But even during sleep the subconscious is still very **active**, processing all the recently gained information and storing it away appropriately. In all, scientific findings estimate that we use only about 10% of our total **brain power**. In purely physical terms, this means that you would need a very large building indeed to house such a **phenomenal amount of information**. But it is all there, embedded deeply into your subconscious. Unfortunately, it may not always be so easy to access a particular piece of information just as and when you need it but the following techniques will give you the tools to make accessing that information much easier so that you can make better decisions in the future.

SHAKESPEARE'S DECISION BOX - TO DO OR NOT TO DO

Consider an important decision you need to make, where you are perhaps feeling a little indecisive and then answer the questions in each box in relation to your current challenge.

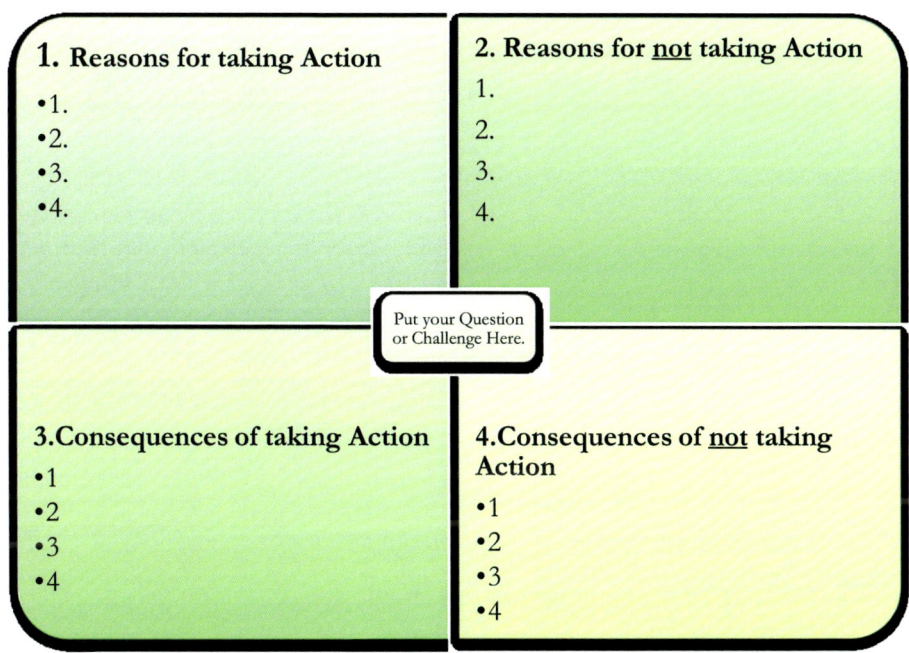

In Box 1 - consider why you **want to change** what you are, what you do or what you own.

In Box 2, - examine why you would do nothing and **make no changes**

Box 3 actually **clarifies your goals**, as well as establishing how you will benefit if you take action. You need to take into account what will change in your life if you do take action. What will you be, do or own which is different to what is in your life now.

Box 4 asks you to consider what will **stay the same** in your life, or what will you lose out on if you take no action.

What this short exercise does uncover is the extent to which you could be missing out on **great opportunities** by not taking action. This simple technique has been proven to have helped numerous people who could not make a decision simply because they perceived the threat of what could go wrong as too powerful to overcome. Writing it down propels the risk into your reality in a conscious logical way.

I recommend that you apply this exercise now, using an example of an **opportunity** that has arisen recently, or an opportunity that you have previously turned down. You can download a copy of this from my website at www.angelawhitlock.com or just write it in the book.

WHAT IF AND WHATEVER

And now let us imagine that box 3 is shouting at you with positive statements, urging you to take action. Excitement is naturally escalating, but perhaps the level of **excitement** has not yet surfaced beyond the fear threshold. This may lead to two considerations:

1. What if…………….…
2. Whatever…………..

Try this little exercise before we discuss these two attitudes;

*Imagine you've left for work and half way there you've realised that you don't have your **mobile phone** with you. You have left it at home. Now consider, what would you do? What action would you take? Write the answer here ....*
or in your journal before you read on.

'WHAT IF' PEOPLE

A great many people fall into this category. The number of 'what ifs' could easily build to the size of a mountain. Once we begin with 'what if' the permutations are endless, backed up by all the usual horror stories of failure, recession and unwarranted risk. A very close cousin to the 'what if' is the 'I told you so', always waiting there in the wings to **remind you** of the uselessness of even attempting to change. If you decided to turn around and go back for your mobile phone in the exercise above, then you are likely to be in this category.

'What if' people remain **steadfastly rooted** where they are. It is virtually impossible for them to move on. They are highly creative in the inexhaustible supply of excuses they can fabricate in order to stifle action. So much so, that if they applied even a small percentage of that **creative energy** to the finding of solutions, they would probably surprise themselves. Typical examples of 'what if' thinking with the mobile phone exercise may be as follows:

A.   What if the babysitter phones me?
B.   What if I don't have enough money with me?
C.   What if anything happens to me?
D.   What if anything happens to anyone else?

The truth is that if you have a phobia or irrational fear in relation to anything at all, then you are probably harbouring 'what if' tendencies. You may not be **consciously** aware of them, but they are clearly present within you.

'WHATEVER' PEOPLE

The 'whatever' people reside in an entirely different mental **landscape**; they have one statement that covers every eventuality:

Whatever happens I'll deal with it

    a.   People know where I am, if they want to contact me

    b.   I've taken sufficient money if I need more its unlikely to be essential

    c.   I'll deal with it - that's part of life

    d.   Whatever happens, people will find me if they need to.

Their philosophy is that simple, that straightforward. They believe: 'whatever life dishes up, we'll take it on board **and 'deal with it'**.

Usually 'whatever' people have a number of different strategies they use to deal with life.

Here is another creative example of 'whatever' thinking that can help to propel you forward in your life and help you make much easier, logical decisions in life.

THE 20/80 RULE

Consider this: For every challenge you face in life, allow yourself just **two minutes** to think about the problem, and **eight minutes** to think about the solution. That means that 20 percent of your time is spent considering the problem and eighty percent thinking about a solution. Sometimes the problem could be extremely serious and distressing. Other problems can be very minor. It may be just a concern as to what you will have for dinner. It really doesn't matter whether the problem is perceived as very serious or just trivial; by applying the exercise you will discover eight different ways of **resolving** your difficulty.

Try this exercise now to a difficulty you may be currently facing, whether the problem involves an opportunity or a challenge. And remember to allow yourself a ratio of just two minutes to think about the problem, and eight minutes to think about the solution.

It may help if you **close your eyes** whilst doing this exercise, simply to shut out outside interference and stimulate creativity. I would recommend a time setting of 10 minutes initially. And notice just how many options you can come up with during that time. You may be **pleasantly surprised**. It is also useful, if you are in a relationship and have a joint decision to make, it can impel you to stop complaining and start taking real action. It will focus both your minds on the real problem and the many possible solutions you can adopt.

My current challenge is ....

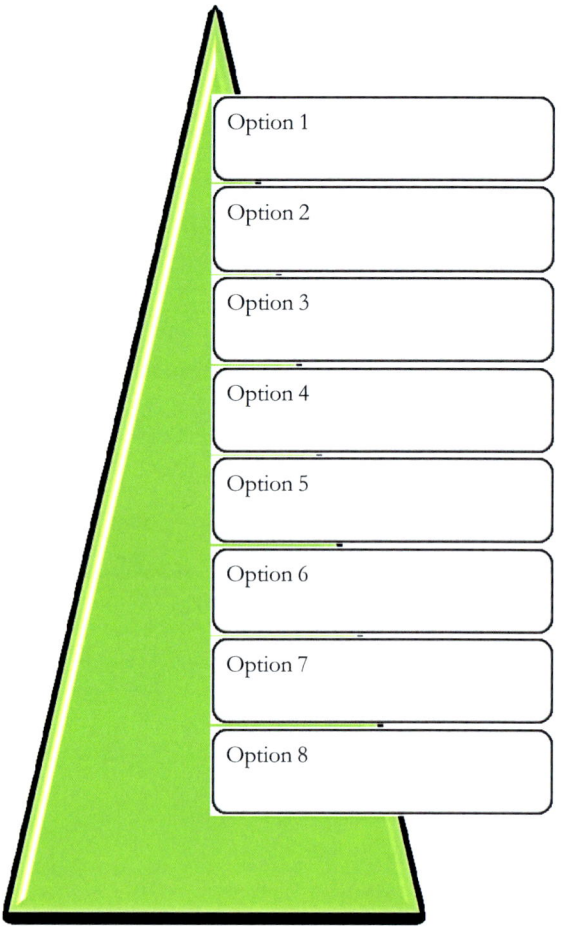

You can download a copy of this from my website at
www.angelawhitlock.com.

A group at one of my seminars recently had a challenge and undertook the above exercise. They exhausted most of the feasible options after six, so initiated a few fun ones, such as throwing themselves on the floor in a tantrum. This was because the group already felt they had sufficient **options** within the first six outcomes.

What undertaking the exercise will achieve is to clarify what options are available to you to act upon and what you can really do about the challenge. You may not be very keen on some of the options, which you may have considered, but they should be included in order to render the risks involved with the first options more palatable.

As a result of carrying out the exercise on a problem of my own, I walked into a solicitor's office early one Monday morning, armed with my eight options and ready to do battle. By the time that option two was introduced from my armoury, the outcome was virtually **agreed**. And I still had another six primed options under my belt. I found it gave me immense confidence to challenge some outdated thinking.

It's well worth taking the time to get thinking creatively with your options. You may be very surprised at the results you can achieve when you apply real **positive thought**.

The technique is also very useful for ridding yourself of any fears. This is because you are confronting the fear head on, and **challenging** it. You are in fact challenging it to: "Come on, give it your best shot, I have 8 options to counter attack that unhealthy thinking with"!

One proven method of accessing the subconscious mind, of asking the pertinent questions and providing the means for **creative decision making**, is through the technique of hypnosis. Unfortunately most of us don't have a handy hypnotherapist or a life coach on tap whenever we need help from our subconscious to make a decision. But what we do have access to are the following tools that you will find very useful:

THE PENDULUM OF CHOICE

The conscious mind is bombarded with information constantly and with this overload of information it can be very difficult to come to the right decision when faced with choices. There's no trickery involved in this exercise. There are no smoke and mirrors. It is purely a **measure** of ideomotor responses, a reflex action of the subconscious translated into bodily movements.

It's a quick and easy technique you can use to engage your subconscious mind, the power house and store of all the information you've every learnt and which will help you whenever you may need aid with your decision making. It's particularly useful as a back-up resource when you feel indecisive about **particular choices** you may need to make. So put that logical, analytical mind to one side for now and open up some right brain thinking. All you require for this simple activity are the following:

* A metal nut and
* A piece of string.

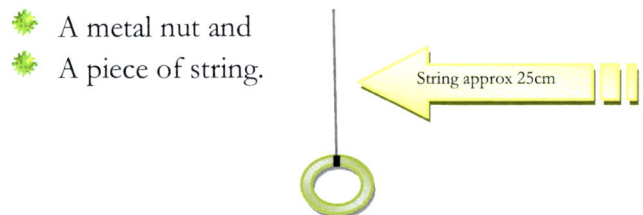

String approx 25cm

Now it's not the kind of 'nut' you see falling out of a pub on a Friday night, or the one you shouldn't go near if you have an allergy. It's the metal variety, the one with a hole in the centre, available at all hardware stores or alternatively you can also use a necklace with a pendant

Simply **tie** the **string** to the **nut** and secure with a knot. The string length should be the approximate measurement from your index finger to your elbow, generally about **25cm**. Together the string and the nut forms a very basic pendulum.

THIS IS HOW IT WORKS:

* Firstly **hold** the pendulum in front of you with your elbow resting on your knee and keeping your hand steady, ask your subconscious to swing the pendulum in the direction of a **'Yes' response**. You need to focus your attention on this question. When the pendulum begins moving, you note the general direction of the swing. This motion is then established as a 'yes' response.

* You then ask your subconscious to swing the pendulum in the direction of a **'No' response**. When the pendulum begins moving, you note the general direction of the swing. This motion is then established as a 'No' response.

* To pre-empt any likelihood of your subconscious being unable to find a response to a question, you then ask it to swing the pendulum, giving **a 'Don't Know'** response. Again, when the pendulum begins moving you note the direction of the swing. This motion is then established as a 'Don't Know' response.

✦ You may then ask your subconscious a **series of questions**, concerning the decision you have to make, to which the answer is either a definite 'yes' or 'no'.

Once you focus your subconscious on the question in hand, the pendulum will then begin moving to give the appropriate answer. Sometimes the movement may be slow and gentle; at other times it may be very rapid. But invariably you will **receive the answer** you require, though the answer will come only after your subconscious has referred to the vast amount of personal information already in store. This is to ensure that it provides you with the **best possible answer** to the question, based on all the information it has available. There's no mysterious force at work or any psychic power involved whatsoever. This is simply a proven way of asking your subconscious mind to provide you with informed responses to the questions surrounding the decision you need to make.

It is simply a widely accepted **experience** called an ideomotor response. It is your very wise and knowledgeable subconscious moving the pendulum, providing what it believes the answer to the question should be. The next time you are faced with a question that is perplexing you, try using this technique. It may clarify how you are feeling about a decision you need to make, and what your intuition is really trying to tell you.

WHAT'S IN THE GARDEN SHED

When I was a child my father seemed to have the answer to every question and problem in the garden shed. You should by now be far better armed to take some **serious action** in your own life and start equipping your own shed.

In this chapter we've discussed the dilemma of risk and reality, and provided you with a number of powerful tools and techniques to help you **prune** your unhealthy thoughts and unleash your creative thinking to perceive the truth about risk and reality related challenges.

- ❊ You have the **Shakespeare's Decision Box,** which will help you to establish the real goal you want to achieve.
- ❊ The **20/80 Rule** will give you added defence against all the 'what ifs' that may try to sabotage your thinking.
- ❊ And finally the **Pendulum of Choice** will allow you to tap deeply into the vast store of information and experience held in your subconscious mind, guiding you towards making the best decisions whenever you need assistance.

The message of this first chapter is simple: Leave regrets behind you in the past, where they belong. It's totally pointless dwelling on missed opportunities, and reflecting negatively on the past. Let the 'if onlys' go too. 'If only I had acted differently... 'If only I had said this or that'. Begin looking to the **NOW**, look to the **FUTURE**. From this point on make the best decisions you can possibly make. Take every opportunity that will benefit you and your personal success.

WALK ON THE GRASS

Chapter 3

The Grass is Greener on the Other Side

WHAT DO YOU BELIEVE?

Almost in disbelief, I shouted to my son, "There's a cow in the garden!"
'Yep, sure there is,' he replied sceptically, hardly lifting his head from his
breakfast bowl. "No, make that two
cows," I shouted, even louder. I continued
to stare out through the window, my eyes
widening: "I don't believe it – the whole
herd is on its way in."

A herd of cows were grazing despondently in a field. The grass was sparse, a short, brown stubble with the texture of straw. Its appearance was neither appetising nor nutritious. Freda, a member of the herd, but evidently not its leader, peered over the fence considering on the condition of the grass on the other side, which looked so much fresher and greener. Unfortunately, there was no **clear way** through to reach the green grass, which was defended by a chicken wire fence and a few wooden posts. "This could hurt," Freda must have considered in her slow bovine way, as she looked to find ways of getting to the grass on the other side of the fence.

It would certainly take serious **focusing and a strong belief** that she could actually break through the fence, before she could commit to attempting to do it. But at 7am one frosty morning, Freda decided the **risk** had become her reality, and that she was going to get through that barrier to better things one way or another. Within ten minutes Freda had managed to break down the fence, and was **walking on the grass** on the other side. Followed by the rest of the herd, she triumphantly set about enjoying the best breakfast she had probably eaten in quite a while.

Now, I understand that cows may not have a reputation for being the most intelligent creatures on earth, but Freda was obviously aware, in defiance of the old adage, that in this case the **grass on the other side** of the fence was certainly **greener**. And from that premise she had formulated a belief that she could somehow get through it, otherwise she would never have attempted the mission. By simply believing that it was possible to achieve her aim, Freda was successful. That's all it took to breach the fence. Perhaps Freda's thought patterns were less complicated than I have given her credit for in this true story, but its clear proof that you don't need superior intelligence in order to believe in yourself. Every **action** begins with the thought that **it is possible** to do something.

To put this into context, a belief is a **thought** that you value as the **truth**. And, as in the story, a belief informs us -

1. why we **can** be, do or own what we want

   Or

2. why we **can't** be, do or own what we want

BELIEVE IN YOURSELF

Beliefs can be divided into various categories, but generally speaking they come under two main headings:

   ❋ **Healthy beliefs** (those that keep us safe and have a positive influence on our lives)

✤ **Limiting beliefs** (those which you may ascribe to, but which have a detrimental and controlling hold on our lives).

We begin structuring our beliefs at a very early age, as soon as we begin the **learning process.** Beliefs are then steadily added to, which increase our personal armoury of defences throughout our growing years. Although we imagine that our beliefs come solely from within ourselves, they can in fact be shaped by many other factors, including:

✤ **Influence** -books or media
✤ **Experience** – events that happen to us
✤ **People** – family, friends, peers, teachers
✤ **Environment** - political, religious, social

Generally healthy beliefs are instilled in us at a very early age. Perhaps you may remember the shock you received the first time you touched something very hot. Afterwards, you very quickly learned to be careful around similar objects or sources of heat.

This awareness enabled you to develop a healthy, protective belief. Unfortunately, people and events can also instil us with many other limiting beliefs, some of which can steal up on us without being noticed.

WHAT'S IN YOUR BELIEF STORE ALREADY?

It may be interesting to discover what your **current belief system** is telling you at the moment. The following exercise should be fun, but may also be quite revealing. Simply read out the listed words below aloud, and then, without thinking too much about it, write down the **first words** that come to mind.

> *Life is*..
>
> *Men are*..
>
> *Women are*...
>
> *Money is*...
>
> *I am*..
>
> *Work is*..
>
> *Success is*...

Now look closely at what you have written down. Are the answers you have given true to your own beliefs? And, if they are, are some of your answers a little more revealing, a little more **surprising** than you might have imagined? Now may be a good time to take a short break and write **some notes** on what you have written before we move on.

SEEDING EVENTS

A seeding event can occur in any number of ways. It can be a belief handed down from members of the family, or can come as a result of a deeply-felt **experience**. The source may also be simply a chance remark that somehow lodges itself firmly in your mind. But however the seed is planted, the effect can be positive or very detrimental to your life unless you recognise the control it has been exercising over you.

Seeding events can be healthy and unhealthy and **influence** your life tremendously, if you allow the unhealthy thoughts that spring naturally from some to keep on growing. Certainly they are likely to affect your levels of personal development, **achievement** and success. By using your own creativity and applying it correctly, you can actually stop the seed from growing so that, in time, it will eventually wither and die.

> *Think back to your childhood: Imagine that you are seven years old and your father offers you the choice of receiving 10p a day or £1 per week pocket money. It's the first time you have experienced owning your own money. Remember, thinking as a child, which option would you choose?*

This actually happened to Jason. The offer was also made to his elder sister who, without any hesitation, immediately insisted on the £1 a week pocket money. However, Jason, believing that it would be better to receive money every day chose the 70p a week option. He could still remember the amusement of his family as they mocked him for making what they considered to be such an obviously poor **choice**.

The light hearted reaction of his family, had in fact deeply affected him, without Jason ever realising it. The belief: 'I'm bad with money' had been sown like a bad seed, eventually taking **root** and growing until it had contaminated every part of his life. That seed of doubt grew over many years into a **self-fulfilling** prophecy that led him to get into a great deal of debt.

The concept of walking on the grass for Jason meant achieving a position of **financial security**, and being in total control of his finances. He wanted so much to start afresh, but lacking confidence in his ability to deal with money issues, he felt incapable of moving on. As with a great many people who are unable to locate the real source of their problems, Jason was never sure if the **memory** of the pocket money incident was really significant in any way.

But the clue was in the clarity with which he could recall the memory – the mind always takes special notice of **important experiences** in our lives, and as a result they stay fast in our memory. That is why we can still recall certain events, which perhaps we didn't think were significant, so clearly after many, many years. Something as apparently innocent as the reaction of his family with regard to his pocket money choice, had the **power** to instil a huge negative belief into Jason that had affected his whole life.

Looking to find a practical **resolution** for his problem, during one of our sessions together, I asked Jason whether he believed that he repaid the money to his debtors via his bank account, or did his creditors take the money from him directly. His initial response was that his creditors took the payments directly. However, when I pointed out that a single phone call to his bank could actually prevent his creditors from taking any more money from his account, a **light** appeared to go on in his mind. He realised that he himself could now choose to pay his debtors, rather than have them take the money from him. And the more he thought about it, the more he realised that even though he was seriously in debt, there were still areas over which he had control. Gradually his old 'money' belief was **realigned** into a belief that he really could begin to take **control** of his finances.

When we discussed the initial seeding event and the process by which he had made his **decision** regarding the pocket money, Jason maintained that given the same options, as an adult but still seeing through his own childish eyes, he would have made exactly the **same choice** again. He insisted that it was what he had genuinely wanted at that time. He hadn't considered the offer in monetary terms at all; he had based his decision on the feeling of excitement he had experienced at the thought of receiving pocket money every day.

He now realised that it wasn't the choice he made that had caused him to doubt himself where money was concerned; it was actually the **reaction** of his family to that choice. That was when the seed of his negative belief had been sown. Jason now realised that no matter how much he might insist to himself that he was good with money, that negative **childhood memory** had set itself up as a barrier, had in fact turned into a belief. Jason was further encouraged to change his long-held belief of being 'bad with money' by undertaking the 'Truth' activity, featured further on in this chapter. As it presently stands, Jason anticipates being debt free in 2011, thirty years earlier than he had previously believed was **possible**.

> *Are there one or more seeding events lodged in your own belief system? Begin to examine them, one at a time. What do you remember whenever you consider a particular problem you may have? What memory springs first into your mind?*

Do you relate to this? You may feel that the memory is insignificant, or has no connection to the problem, but if it comes to mind quickly then it may be still very much alive for you. Try applying the following 'Truth' exercise to any seeding event which may still be **vivid** in your memory. It may help you to disconnect the hold it has on you.

Nothing is ever small or insignificant to the mind. Take a simple remark, such as, 'why did you do such a stupid clumsy thing'. We've all heard similar remarks, probably applied to ourselves from time to time. But **imagine** if you heard that same remark over and over again, spoken or shouted at you with real venom or spite. Or if you heard it from someone you deeply **respected**; perhaps it might have been said to you when you were feeling particularly sensitive and vulnerable. How easily, do you think, you could begin to believe that you were actually really stupid or even clumsy. That is typically how many of these unhealthy belief seeds are sown. Often a remark or observation may even be well intended, but if the mind, which takes everything very literally, translates it negatively, the seed that grows from it can cause harm. That's why it's so important to recognise it, and learn to realign it so that your perception and the control it has changes. It could be the vital obstacle that is barring your way to personal success and real achievement.

THE TRUTH IS OUT THERE

Beliefs can chain you to a prison cell wall of despair, or they can release you to fly at will, free like a bird. Beliefs carry tremendous power, for both good and ill. Let's now examine ways to use them so that you can begin walking on the grass, and moving towards much greater personal success and achievement.

Using your creative abilities fully, write out, illustrate or read out aloud the details of a significant event. It may be an experience you had in the past, but one which still remains very fresh in your memory. It could be one of those insistent memories that perhaps turn over and over in your mind, but you don't really know why.

Triggering event (what actually happened)

-
-

Reflection (what did you do about it)

-
-

Unhealthy response (what made it negative at the time)

-
-

Truth (what was really occurring)

-
-

Healthy response (On reflection would you have reacted differently)

-
-

Imagine yourself now applying a healthy response to that memorable event; spend a few moments re-running or rewinding the memory surrounding it, and then imagine the most **pleasing outcome** possible to the event.

We can't travel back in time, but what we can do is apply the learning, use the **experience** gained from past events to deal with any similar situation which may arise in the future. By using your creative thinking ability you have all the means necessary to shape your own outcome to any situation you may find yourself in from now on. Already, without realising it, you are building up your deposits of creative thinking, **investing** them in the bank of your mind and developing an entirely new way of thinking in the future.

Are you the quiet one in a gathering of family or friends, insisting you are a listener rather than a talker?
Perhaps wanting to join in the conversation but not feeling like you have anything of value to say?

Amanda was a vibrant, confident person. She never set out to be the life and soul of the party, but had a reputation for being fun to be around. She was very **comfortable** in familiar company, in small groups and in one to one situations. But whenever she found herself in an unfamiliar social situation with more than four people present, she immediately became quiet and withdrawn. She was a very intelligent girl, and was quite aware of how unreasonably these situations affected her. For years she attempted to **rationalise** it to herself, making herself believe that her reticence was simply due to the fact that she was a very good listener, but not a talker.

On one particular occasion her partner attempted to bring her into the general family conversation. She reacted very angrily, practically snarling at him, obviously annoyed at what he had deliberately tried to do. Amanda **realised** though, that her **reaction** had been unreasonable and unfair towards her partner, who had been very offended by it. She had also noticed how similar reactions to the same kind of social situations in the workplace were achieving little to advance her career. She wanted desperately to **change**, but was finding it impossible to do so. In discussing her problem, she told me about one of her earliest childhood memories. Amanda recounted that she could have been no more than two-years-old, but was able to clearly recall sitting around the dinner table with her elder siblings. She **remembered** that they had all been chattering, and that she too had wanted very much to join in. But, for some reason, she'd begun to feel very uncomfortable, sensing with her two-year-old mind that her opinion on anything would not be **important** because she was so little. She could also vaguely recall that her sister, who had been 15 years older than Amanda, had told her to be quiet, although she could not recall having said much, if anything at all.

She'd never considered this memory as important or significant in any way. But when she'd applied it to 'The Truth is Out There' exercise, and followed the recommendation to imagine how she could have behaved differently in the circumstances, she realised that there was really **nothing** she could have **changed** at the time. She had been far too young to really understand why she had felt as she had done whilst sitting around that table. But now that she could review it as an adult, with full self awareness, she realised that her **subconscious** mind was taking her back, albeit very subtly, to that event and the uncomfortable feelings she had experienced every time she was in a group resembling that family gathering, which had sat around the dinner table so many years ago.

When she became fully **aware** of the memory, and rationalised it, she realised that nothing she had said or done on that day justified the belief that no-one wanted to listen to her or her opinion. After all, she had been just two-years-old. The seed that had been sown in her came as a result of a casual remark from her older sister, which had lodged itself firmly inside her mind. Now, having confronted and understood the event, she could **discard it** and move on.

TIME FOR THE REFUSE COLLECTORS

In order to let go of anything unwanted, including the influence of negative events, you have to find a way of **disposing** of it forever. One way is to consider what you would really like to do with that heavy baggage you may have been carrying around for so long. It's simply a burden. You already know that there's nothing in it that you need, so why should you continue to carry it? Instead, why not put it out with the rest of the rubbish that you don't need? Why not **free up some space** and allow your creativity to begin filling your mind with entirely new thoughts, entirely new possibilities.

Some people on completing the exercise take great pleasure in **tearing up the paper** they've written on, before throwing the pieces in a bin. Others, to ensure that those negative beliefs really do disappear forever, prefer to **shred** or burn it. It really doesn't matter how you get rid of the old way of thinking, as long as you do. Only when you really let go of the tainted events of the past which you cannot change will you ever learn to be in control of your future.

THE PLACE YOU WERE BORN COULD BE LIMITING YOUR SUCCESS

> *People will seldom rise above their own opinion of themselves.*

Many people have **risen to success** and high achievement from impoverished backgrounds. The difference between these people and others, who grew up in a similar area, and with a similar background, is that the successful people had a focus and a greater opinion of themselves. They believed they could **achieve success**. Of course, we are all influenced to some extent by our immediate environment. But so often, particularly if your upbringing has been against the backdrop of a poor council estate, or if you have experienced real extremes of poverty, your **belief system** embraces the old and dull conviction that, 'People like me don't achieve successes, my opinion isn't valid'. And, of course, if that is truly what you believe, then you won't achieve success. How could you? In fact the only way you will ever achieve success, is to challenge that belief, and to change it.

> *Do you believe that where you were born affects your ability to be successful?*
> *Would you happily talk to a Managing Director of a major company about your background or would you hide it?*

In order to achieve any level of success, it is necessary to absolutely **challenge the belief** and break the rule you may have made that your destiny has already been decided by environment and background, and that success and achievement are far beyond your reach. It is, after all, a totally unreasonable belief. If I had the space, I could fill this book with the names of people who could verify that fact.

For the list of those born in poverty, inflicted by debilitating illness, or who came from a loveless, disadvantaged background, but went on to achieve tremendous success and bring about **massive** social change, is endless. Your birthright and background cannot hold you back or deny the fulfilment of your real potential. Only you can do that.

> *Imagine what life would be like if you were born to a more privileged life?*
> *How would you think differently now?*

Use your innate creativity to take you where you **really want to go.** Challenge your thinking with any of the activities in this chapter because you too deserve to be happy. And, remember, you have as much right as anyone to be successful.

SUPERSTITIONS

How many superstitions are borne out of unhealthy beliefs? Most people are probably aware of the superstition claiming that it's unlucky to walk under ladders. Now, let's just consider that for a moment. Isn't it more feasible that the superstition is borne out of **simple common sense**, rather than any supernatural heritage? After all, if you see a ladder propped up against a wall, there is a very strong chance that someone may be on it or working from above. Painters, window cleaners and builders spring to mind. It therefore follows that there is statistically a much greater chance of something dropping on your head if you walk under the ladder, than there would be if you took the trouble to walk around it.

The unconscious absorption of many other superstitions, similar to this, can have the effect of seeding a negative thought in your mind. And, like any **seed planted** in the ground, the seed will eventually grow in to a full sized plant. To continue the analogy, the plant will then flower and begin passing its seed to other soil until it begins to grow in other minds too. Just consider how many superstitions were never yours at all!

PLANTING NEW BELIEFS

It is possible to challenge any **established belief** once you are aware of the detrimental effect that the belief is exercising on you. Spend a few moments now writing, illustrating or simply reading out loud any limiting beliefs you may have that you feel may be holding you back. I would suggest that you refer to the related activity you did earlier in this chapter, and perhaps begin expanding on it.

> *Life is*...
> *Men are*..
> *Women are*...
> *Money is*...
> *I am*...
> *Work is*..
> *Success is*...

There are also some very simple techniques you can apply in order to address beliefs. A few typical examples are as follows:

YOUR COMPUTER PASSWORD

If you regularly use a computer, then it is likely that you need a password in order for it to become operational. Examine your **password** carefully; it will give you an insight into what you are currently focusing on. And then consider a new password, something that has a very **positive message**. Create the new password by using a word or phrase that has special meaning for you, or a combination that is likely to give you inspiration. If you have already formed a personal goal, select a password that will reinforce that goal, e.g. IamConfident2010.

YOUR MOBILE PHONE

Add positive words to the stored names of your friends in your **mobile phonebook** list, so that every time you look to dial a number you'll be reminded to reinforce your positive beliefs. The following examples should give you some ideas:

- John on your call list becomes: John – u can do it

- Amy becomes: 'Amy - admires me

It's such a simple technique, which takes hardly any effort or time. You could do it right now. You may be pleasantly surprised at how effectively your beliefs can be strengthened by the repetition of a positive word or phrase displayed before you, each time a friend or family member rings you.

SURROUND YOURSELF WITH POSITIVE IMAGES

If your limiting belief is related to concerns about your money handling ability, try putting some **foreign currency in a photo frame** and keep it in easy view. Foreign currency tends to look more exotic and interesting, and this framed 'portrait' will remind you of the importance of keeping hold of your money.

Constant unconscious reference to the 'portrait' will also **inspire** your creative thinking to find the solution to ridding yourself of the limiting belief.

TURN IT ALL UPDSIDE DOWN

A client confided that he had retained an ambition to buy a classic sports car for over 20 years. However, he admitted, he could not possibly see any way in which he would ever have sufficient money to buy one, because  he could not save enough money and he had too many other responsibilities. My suggestion was that he turned the premise **on its head:** Instead of wondering how he could save the money, he should begin to take back money from those to whom he was freely giving it. He appeared baffled at first, and then he began to understand. He started with small adjustments. For instance, he stopped buying sandwiches at the same shop every day, and instead made sandwiches himself at home. He began to notice his spending habits more, realising that many of them were unreasonable and wasteful. He **consciously stopped spending** money when he really didn't need to, or buying things that he really didn't require.

Every time he resisted an impulse to spend money for no good reason, he kept the money and put it aside, accumulating a fund for the express purpose of buying that classic sports car. He didn't skimp, or deprive the family finances in any way, so there was no feeling of guilt or meanness involved. He simply stopped spending unnecessarily. In fact, if anyone was deprived, it was the stores and shops which he used to patronise regularly. But that was not his problem. Within two years he had **acquired** sufficient funds with which to purchase the longed-for car. The day he bought the vehicle, he sat outside on the lawn and gazed at it for a very long time, scarcely believing that his **ambition** had finally been fulfilled. He could not have been more happy or proud. He truly was walking on the grass; well sitting on it anyway.

SUCCESS JOURNAL

Each time you challenge a tired old belief and sow a new positive seed in its place, write down or turn it into a poem and illustrate your feelings of achievement in your own **success journal**. Recording successes in this way will be a very effective way of reflecting and reminding yourself of your achievements so far, as well as giving you the confidence to achieve so much more. And look after your **new seed,** nurture it as you would care for a flower seed you had sown yourself. As with anything uncared for in nature, without your persistent attention, the seed is likely to just wither and die. Help it to **grow** and develop, and delight in the knowledge that soon it will be strong enough to stand firmly on its own.

BALLOONS

Another very enjoyable and creative method of dispersing unhealthy and unwanted beliefs can be achieved through the simple device of a balloon. The method: inflate the balloon and, using a coloured marker pen, write down every negative thought you wish to get rid forever of on the skin of the balloon. Then, when you are quite ready, begin to visualise yourself **breaking free of** whatever restrictive beliefs you think may be holding you back from success. Once you have made a total commitment to get rid of these beliefs forever, **pop** the **balloon** with a pin or sharp point. As the balloon explodes feel the chains of the old beliefs breaking forever, setting you completely free. Quite often, a wonderful feeling of peace and utter relief accompany the end of this exercise.

THREE MAGIC MEMORIES

To start you off, can you recall three of the most **magical memories** in your life, times and experiences that were incredibly special to you? Perhaps there was one outstanding moment when you **laughed** so much with joy that you actually cried. You may have had many more magic memories, but write down three of the most memorable ones:

Magic Memories
1.
2.
3.

Record these magic memories in your journal, and refer to them often, especially when you may be feeling low or a little sad. Read through the details thoroughly. Not only will the memory put a smile on your face as you **recapture** those wonderful memories, but you will be reminded that such times and moments can come again in the future.

BACK TO THE GARDEN SHED

In this chapter we have more tools for the garden shed. We've discussed **beliefs** and the devastating effect that unhealthy beliefs can exercise over your life. We have also discussed ways and means by  which they may be **challenged**, using a number of very simple activities. And, more importantly, we have examined ways in which these tired, old limiting beliefs can be replanted with healthy beliefs, thus **sowing new seeds**, which will bring about the changes you desire to ensure much more fulfilment and personal success in your life.

* If you find it difficult to believe in yourself, even though your friends constantly tell you how brilliant you are, your lack of confidence may simply stem from a **seeding event**, of which you may not be fully aware. Apart from using all the techniques already set out in order to rid yourself of this stifling limitation, let the praise of your friends be reflected by using positive words or phrases on your **mobile phonebook list**.

* Remember our perception is our reality. In order to raise your opinion of yourself, it is necessary to change your perception to a truer reality as explained in the **Truth** exercise.

* Surround yourself with **positive images**; capture your successes and positive feelings in a **journal or notebook**. The more your

perception begins to change, the more quickly your limiting belief begins to crumble and then eventually wither away.

* Start popping those **balloons** and explode all those negative beliefs. Re-acquaint yourself with your treasured **magic moments**, and allow your creativity and your intuition to set to work and give you back more control of your life.

Chapter 4

You Are What You Think You Are

BE AWARE OF YOUR THOUGHTS

The kids were rampaging through the house. Their father, at his wits end, shouted loudly at them: "Stop or you'll fall!" His wife immediately reprimanded him for giving voice to the negative idea of falling. He reacted by yelling at the top of his voice in the general direction of the kids: "WALK!" Almost in immediate response, the kids stopped running and calmed down. But now the dog sprang into action, bounding out of his bed and dashing towards his lead. "Perhaps next time, it might be better if you spell it out", the man's wife advised. Words can be very misleading at times!

Have you ever wondered why it is that when you buy something, for example, a new car, you immediately begin noticing other cars of the same model, make or colour, until it appears that every other car on the road is exactly the same as yours? It's as though they have just suddenly sprung up from nowhere. These cars have always been there, of course, but you simply never **noticed** them before. The same thing happens when, to use another example, you may decide to begin dieting. All of a sudden there is nothing else in the world but references to dieting. You hear people discussing it in shops, cafes, on the buses. It seems to be the main subject of every television and radio programme. You can't open a newspaper or magazine without reading an article about dieting.

It should come as no **real surprise**, of course, when you seem for a time to become obsessed by one thought or subject. It was what our mind was thinking about, what it was **concentrated** on when we bought the new car, or decided to diet. And the mind will always completely focus on whatever our thoughts are directed towards.

Clinical Studies have concluded that we have in excess of 60,000 **thoughts** each a day. Now, you have to admit, that's an awful lot of thoughts racing through your mind. Further research has found that as many as 75% of those thoughts are likely to be negative in nature. Is it any wonder, therefore, that we sometimes feel a little stressed or in low spirits. That 75% or so equates to an average of;

45,000 negative thoughts a day.

It is also reasonable to assume that the top 10% of those thoughts that are processing through your mind during any given day will attract the **most attention**. Think of it like this: Out of a group of children in a classroom, one child is jumping up and down, waving her hands in the air and shouting: 'Miss! Miss!' There may be a great many children in the classroom, possibly 30 or more, but where do you imagine the schoolteacher's attention will fall. The mind will always focus on the thoughts that demand the most attention, whether they are positive or negative.

I would imagine that by now, you already have some **understanding** of how the process works; when you were buying that new car or focusing on the diet, you automatically promoted those thoughts to the top of your thought list. In short, you concentrated all of your attention on them, so that the mind became, for a short time at least, totally preoccupied with them to the exclusion of everything else.

How many pink cars have you seen in the last week?

It's probable that you can't recall seeing many pink cars, if any at all. However, I am suggesting that in the next seven days you particularly begin to notice pink cars, and will begin seeing more of them. In fact it's probable that you may be surprised to notice how many there actually are on the road. This is because I have now **drawn your attention** specifically to pink cars, and you will automatically find yourself subconsciously looking for them.

This is an example of your cognitive thought processes at work, escalating thoughts that have been heavily impressed on to you or thoughts that are **particularly important** to you, to the top of the brain chain, whilst at the same time downgrading thoughts that have little relevance or seem unimportant. It's similar to the process of a manager prioritising tasks which are considered urgent or immediate, whilst putting to one side matters that can be resolved without a time frame.

Because your thoughts interpret things very literally, they can sometimes appear quite tricky, and even dangerous. This is because your thoughts will always **give attention** to whatever you are currently focusing on, whether it is positive or negative. Here's an example of what I mean: Have you ever left the house on a frosty or icy day, determined that you do 'not fall' or slip. And then, moments later, you find yourself sprawled out embarrassingly on the path or pavement. Having been so determined 'not to fall', you are now irritated and very upset, so much so that you cannot actually believe that you did.

The reason for this is in the way your **brain interpreted** that determination not to fall. As you completely focused your attention on NOT falling, automatically an image of falling was sent to the brain. It was probably a strong image, because it was driven by a real fear and anxiety. You may also have been silently saying, as well as thinking to yourself at the same time, "don't fall". Unfortunately the brain, fuelled by the image it had received, was concerning itself with the more interesting element of falling, and scarcely took notice of the 'don't' aspect, which it failed to convert in time. In essence, because all of your **attention** was focused on the one thing you didn't want to happen, your mind kindly obliged by ensuring that it did.

There are many similar examples of brain misconception: Parents are particularly adept at directing their children towards doing exactly what they don't want them to do. Whenever they cry: 'Don't run or you'll fall,' there is a fair chance that the child will immediately topple over. At this point the parent would normally scold the child for not listening to them. Unfortunately the child did listen, but all the child's brain heard were the words 'run' and 'fall'. And that's exactly what was arranged. If you're a parent and you're beginning to feel somewhat guilty at this point, I'm sorry but it is true.

We spend a great deal of time being told what to do, and also when to do it. **Walking on the grass** has been specifically designed to point out that there are other ways of ensuring our own safety and well-being. It's about breaking your rules, making your **own choices** and decisions, and being in control of your own life and destiny.

BAND OF CHANGE

A really useful creative tool to help you towards greater awareness of your negative emotions is the **Band of Change**. This technique provides a method of distraction away from unconstructive thoughts and feelings by replacing the energy of unhelpful thinking.

❋ Simply place a normal **elastic band on your wrist**. It's generally more effective if you place the band on the left wrist if you are right-handed and vice-versa if you are left handed. Easily hidden under clothing, you wear the band as you would a bracelet.

The next step is to begin to become **aware** of any negative thought or feeling. Then as soon as a negative thought comes into your mind, **flick the band** against your skin. You don't have to flick it hard or hurt yourself in any way. As you do so, consciously replace the thought with a positive one. An example might be when you are the car or on a bus: instead of thinking 'why do drivers do such stupid things like putting lipstick on or eating' when you notice someone doing so, reverse it to 'what another driver does is out of my control, what they do is up to them'. Before you know it, the negative thought has dissolved.

Negative thoughts, of course, come **in many** guises, and are sometimes difficult to detect. It could be a simple judgemental thought on **someone who is** passing by or on another motorist when you are driving in your car. Or it could be a recurring thought, looping around continuously as it circles your mind. One way to identify a negative thought is that it usually makes you feel uncomfortable. But whatever the negative, unhelpful or unproductive thought may be, the **Band of Change** can greatly help to break its pattern.

After using this technique for 21 days, you will find yourself becoming more **acutely aware** of negative, unhelpful thoughts, or even being judgemental because you have been consciously watching for them to appear. You are in a way training yourself by th**e use of the band** to react immediately to negative thought patterns; each time you flick the band you are in effect asking your unconscious mind to replace the negative thought with a positive one. The simplicity of the band also allows you to be discreet about what you are actually doing.

What may **surprise** you when you begin using this technique is the realisation of how many negative thoughts you actually do have. You also learn that even the most positive people have to deal with some measure of negativity in their thinking. But what is really important to remember is that every single negative thought that you do not dismiss has within it the **potential** to provide the greatest obstacle to your personal success.

As with everything, the more you use the technique, the more accomplished you will become at distracting yourself from unhelpful thoughts and hurtful feelings and as your awareness increases you will no longer need the physical band.

WHAT IS A WORD WORTH?

One of the most significant words to reduce from your vocabulary is the word *'Don't'*. It is possibly one of the words most misunderstood and wrongly translated by the mind as I mentioned earlier, particularly where internalising your thoughts are concerned. Perhaps it's the contradiction between the action word **'do'** and the negative word **'not'** that confuses the thought processes. But the fact is that use of this word when relating to an action can produce the most adverse and opposite effect of what was intended.

In order to avoid this, instead of saying, for example: 'Don't run', which is often translated in a child's mind as 'run like hell', focus on the **actual activity** you are **recommending**, which may be: 'Walk slowly'. You'll soon notice what a **difference** it makes, particularly in the responses of your children. There may also be instilled within us an element of childhood rebellion against the word, which reminds us of constantly being told what we could not do, rather than what would be good for us to do.

This is especially useful in a working environment. Telling people what you want them to do, rather than what you don't want them to do, will inevitably get much better results.

SHUDDA, CUDDA OR WUDDA

Some other words which need to be culled from your vocabulary in order to improve your thinking processes are: *'should have','* *could have'* and *'would have'*. These words may have been a large part of the standard language of our childhood, but now as adults it really is time to discard them. Initially the 'should', 'could' and 'would' family served us well in developing childhood; they were primarily safety words that protected us from making the wrong decision, doing the wrong thing or from hiding behind excuses when we wouldn't admit to being in the wrong.

However, as adults we know that when we make a decision we must also take **full responsibility** for it, whether we 'should have', 'could have' or 'would have' done everything differently with the advantage of hindsight. Because all these expressions are formed in the past tense, no amount of focusing on them can actually change or alter anything because the events and circumstances that triggered them are now gone and may not ever be recalled. They serve no other purpose than to encourage us to analyse past actions, or past decisions, leading us down the long and winding pathway to negative reflection and thinking.

❀ I *shudda* took that job

❀ I *shudda* been more careful

❀ I *cudda* been successful

❀ I *cudda* been an airline pilot

❀ I *wudda* been picked for the team if only …….

❀ I *wudda* got that medal if ……..

A close relative of the 'shudda', 'cudda' and 'wudda' family is the expression 'if only'. Usually accompanied by a deep sigh, 'If only' is a reflective word, often associated with sadness and regret. Typical examples of the expression are: 'If only' circumstances had been different', 'if only' this or that had not happened. The truth is, however, that we can never really know that if these **imagined perfect circumstances** had been present, whether the outcome of your action or decision would have been any better. For example, let's take the following example: 'if only' you had left the house five minutes earlier, you would not have missed the train'. But, for all anyone knows, 'if only' you had left the house five minutes earlier, you might have been hit by a truck.

And another mischievous thought is, 'if only he did this then I could do that' when referring to the actions another person 'shudda' undertaken.

But the truth is that you have no control over anyone's actions, only **your own.** So allow other people to make their own choices, which will allow you to make yours.

The point is that 'if only' is another expression with its roots in the past, reflecting only on what might have occurred. But whatever **shudda, cudda or wudda** happened, in fact it never did or never could happen. So if all the 'if onlys' in the world can never change a moment of what has already passed, why not simply let the past go and stop dwelling on it? It may be useful when you next find yourself reflecting on these pointless past tense thoughts to refer back to Chapter 2, and examine again the **20/80 rule.** Isn't it more sensible to spend eighty percent of your thinking time on the solution to the problem and 20 percent on the problem, rather than the other way around?

A real **conscious effort** to be aware of your usage of these pointless expressions will soon reduce their impact, and rid of you of another deceitful aspect of negative thinking.

> *So ask yourself now, are you waiting for someone else to take action before you can move on in life and be successful?*

By focusing on your own destiny, and turning your own unhealthy thinking around, you may be very surprised at how **positive events** just start to happen for you.

HABITS

The first time I was asked about my habits, I confidently said that I didn't have any. It didn't take very long for me to find out that I had been both very foolish, and very wrong. But the truth was that I genuinely wasn't **consciously aware** of these habits. After all, I'd always prided myself in never doing the same thing twice, and having so much variety in my life. How then, I wondered, could I possibly have any habits?

Well, if you too believe that you are completely habit free, welcome to a reality check. It's not a question of whether you have habits or not, it's more a matter of how many and what kind of habits they are? To discover your own habits, start to **make notes in** your **journal or notebook**, logging the activities that you repeat every day; perhaps you can begin with the time you set for your alarm clock in the morning.

Now consider the following: What are your first actions in getting out of bed? Do you bathe or shower? Do you have a routine for getting dressed? Do you brush your teeth before getting dressed, or after? Perhaps you don't brush your teeth at all? If that's the case, I can recommend you to another e-book entitled: "How to Lose Friends and Affect Them for Life!" I imagine you are beginning to get the point. The **truth** is that every single one of us has habits. We develop habits that govern our domestic life, our work, our hobbies and interests and our social life. We are all, in fact, very much creatures of habit. But not all habits are bad, of course, some are vital in **bringing structure** and a sense of security into our lives, the danger only starts when habits become rules.

The following sentiment sums up how many people feel about their habits:

> *'It's not a habit it's just comfortable, and I've always done it like that.'*
> *And, when questioned about the possibility of changing the habit:*
> *"Ah but..... I can't because.........."*

In order to break bad habits, you first need to **become aware** that you have them. To do this you need to begin to identify your own habits, and their patterns. You can start by making a note in your journal or notebook of the things you do every day, or even those things you do regularly or periodically. Establishing exactly what habits you have, is the first step towards changing or breaking them.

> *Do you always go to the same restaurant, bar or cafeteria? Why not have a change? Try visiting a different one. Do you use the same supermarket? Perhaps you're missing out on better quality goods or cheaper prices. Why not try a different one?*

But what has changing your habits to do with using your creativity for personal success, you may be wondering? The fact is that the more you hold on to old ideas, old ways of doing things, and old ways of looking at the world, the greater the barriers become to the creation of new solutions to the old familiar problems. We've probably all met people who don't like change, who hang on to old ways of life and old ways of looking at things, and, more often than not, old problems. They've always been present historically: They are usually the last to admit to the **benefits** of inventing the wheel, of horseless carriages, electricity, central heating and mobile phones. They don't like change because they fear it, but more than that they fear the initial effort they may have to make in order for their lives to be improved by **adapting** to those changes.

Of course, with every change there is initially a level of discomfort. We've all felt it, from the trepidation of that first day at a new school, to starting a new job. But the discomfort is the **small price** we have to pay for making those changes that will eventually enable us to overcome greater challenges, lead us towards a better life and **greater success**, and fulfil our potential as human beings. And it's no different with changing your habits. Be assured though, that the feeling of discomfort is a **good sign**. It means that you are motivating your creativity to move you out of the unhealthy, unhelpful and negative thinking, and closer to achieving your own personal achievement and fulfilment.

Don't remain stuck in the past until you find your feet have taken root and you can't even lift them up!

THE 'AHH BUT' PRINCIPLE

The 'Ahh but' response is the principle of so many of the reasons that prevent us from taking **positive action**, whether it's applying for promotion, or a pay rise at work, or simply because we believe we do not have the time to do something. You'll recognise a few of the examples we've already discussed in other chapters:

 "I can't do that"

🌿 "But what if"

🌿 "Ahh but"

The 'Ah but' response is a **wonderful excuse**, and the perfect tool for the use of people who set themselves up for failure before they even begin to do anything at all.

> *For some time Miranda had suffered from panic attacks. In desperation she had tried every kind of therapy to rid herself of the terrifying feelings she constantly endured. But nothing ever seemed to help her. In her constant state of anxiety she was unaware of the persistent pattern that had formed in her approach to all these therapies; each time she undertook a different course of therapy, she would think to herself, subconsciously: "Ahh but, it can't work because nothing else has". It was a self-fulfilling prophecy that ensured that no amount of therapy on earth would ever help Miranda.*

It became evident that two related thought patterns were at work in Miranda's case. Firstly, the 'ah but' response, which was preparing her for failure on every occasion, and the self sabotage which came from the fact that she had no belief that any therapy could actually help her. Unconsciously, Miranda wasn't ready for the possibility of being **successful and happy**, a state she might well have achieved once her panic attacks had ceased because her first decision would be to deal with the loveless partnership she was in. It may sound harsh and rather strange, but some people **unconsciously** cling on to curable illness because they are unable to face up to life squarely without a tangible excuse for being incapable of dealing with it.

The 'Ah But' people can also be **staggeringly creative.** They can provide a hundred different reasons why something is not feasible, or won't work. Imagine the **wonderful possibilities** if that creativity was applied to a hundred different reasons why it was feasible, or why it would work? If you recognise any of the 'ah but' or self-sabotage signals in yourself, perhaps it's time to build a bonfire.

BUILD A BONFIRE!

Research confirms that one of the greatest killers of the 20th Century is stress. I could write a whole new volume on what stress actually is, but that wouldn't help you to deal with the consequences of this modern killer. It may sound **simplistic**, but it is nevertheless true to say that one of the first steps for dealing with the effects of stress is to **change the pattern of your thoughts**, and stop focusing on the bad memories and unpleasant experiences of the past. The past is dead and gone, and nothing you can do can ever change that. Instead begin to recognise those negative thoughts and habits that have been keeping you standing still, or worse still taking you backwards.

Begin to use your **imagination** to visualise a better and much more positive future. There is no doubt about it, you really can fulfil your **potential** and achieve great things simply by thinking about what you really want in creative ways. Remember, what your thoughts focus on the most is what your mind pays attention to. Start **attracting** the things you want, the life you want, simply by thinking about them more positively and creatively and turning those thoughts into real actions.

Change doesn't always take place immediately. Sometimes the meaning of a word, phrase or sentence you've heard spoken, or a thought that flits through your mind doesn't always make any sense at the moment it first occurred to you. But perhaps several days, weeks or even months later, it becomes clarified for you in a kind of **enlightening** revelation. The mind can, indeed, work in very mysterious ways. But if you have been reading this book with the intention of improving the **reality of your own life**, I can assure you that some change has already taken place, no matter how major or minor it might have been. Hopefully you have been making **notes and illustrations** on the various techniques and exercises already presented, as suggested. If so, I now recommend that you look back over those records and notice how much your thinking may already have changed. You may be rather surprised.

The fact remains that you have two choices of how you will now proceed in life: You will either **use the learning** and experience that you have already gained in order to create a new future for yourself, or you will **continue** to carry around your old rules, negative thoughts and unreasonable beliefs, so that you remain exactly where you are now.

Of course, nobody deliberately and wilfully carries around heavy objects that are old and useless, and that serve no purpose whatsoever. And to give you some kind of indication of the weight of the load you may be carrying, I'd like you to imagine that every single negative thought you carried around with you was represented by a **single plank** of wood. How many planks of wood, I wonder, would you actually have? And how long would you be able to carry the entire load of them before you buckled under the weight? I imagine that very soon you would require the use of a very large truck, if you persisted in carrying them with you.

So, what are we going to do with all these negative thoughts, all these planks of wood? One thing we do know about wood, is that it burns very well. The logical answer then, to rid you of this mountain of **dead wood** is, of course, to burn it on a bonfire.

Now, using your creative mind, I'd like you to **imagine constructing that bonfire**. Remember every individual negative thought or experience you can bring to mind is represented by one single plank of wood. How high, do you think, your bonfire would be? What shape would it resemble?

Begin to see yourself piling up the bonfire with those dead planks of wood and, when you are quite ready to rid yourself of every single plank, imagine setting fire to it. Now, see it burning, feel the intense heat of the flames. You can even put your hands before it to keep you warm. Notice the fine **crackling noise the wood** *makes as it burns; notice the smell, the smoke. The more you can use your creative mind to imagine that fiercely burning bonfire, the quicker the planks of wood will be consumed by the flames, leaving nothing but the charred cinders of your past negativity. You can build your bonfire now or when you're ready. There's no need to wait until November 5th. But I can assure you that when you have finished burning all of your dead wood, you will feel a* **wonderful sense of relief.** *And what's more you really will be walking on the grass.*

FREEDOM TO BREAK YOUR OWN RULES

I asked a young client of mine to define what **freedom** actually was, and what the word meant to him. His response came very quickly: "Just to do anything you want". I smiled, and then the grown up in me was forced to question his statement by asking: "Do you mean without fear of retribution?" I didn't communicate my final thought, "And preferably without murdering or hurting anyone in the process." I hope that the idea of harming others was not included in his idea of what freedom meant, but who knows what goes on in the teenage mind!

Of course, we all have to live within the confines of the laws that govern us, and I'm sure my young client was fully aware of that when he answered that freedom is to **do anything you want**. But in the simplicity of his answer, he had formulated the way in which creativity really works. There are **no rules** governing creativity. Each individual is able to use his or her own mind, perception and imagination in any way they choose in order to create their own reality. If the first attempt at doing something doesn't work, do it a different way until it does. Lack of education, a poor background or limited resources are no barrier to the truly **inspired** and **creative** mind.

When you are truly tapped into a **vein of creative inspiration**, ideas can fly out of you like machine gun bullets. Most may miss the target and be ultimately discarded, but sooner or later one bullet will find the bullseye. As an example of what I mean, James Dyson recently wrote in an article that he had produced over 5000 prototypes of his famous vacuum cleaner before he discovered the one that actually worked. Have **faith in your ideas**, start to recognise and **break your own rules**, and keep going until you discover what really works for you.

I had a mental block, and badly needed some creative inspiration. I walked into the garden, and noticing the children's trampoline, began bouncing up and down on it, thoroughly enjoying myself. Then I became aware that a fisherman on the opposite side of the river bank was looking at me. Immediately I stopped bouncing and feeling very sheepish, climbed down from the trampoline. The light-hearted feeling I had experienced as I bounced on the trampoline rapidly drained away, and was replaced by uncomfortable feelings of negativity as I wondered: What must he think of me? How embarrassing! It's just not the done thing for an adult to be bouncing on a kids' trampoline! Then the thought suddenly occurred to me: 'It's my house, my garden, my trampoline!' The only thing that was preventing me from enjoying myself were my own rules that told me that grown-up people shouldn't play on a kids' trampoline. So I broke my own rules and carried on bouncing.

Time to Relax

Distraction and fun can really **free-up a blocked mind**, and I started to laugh to myself as I imagined the fisherman later telling the story of the 'mad woman' bouncing on a trampoline. Even if no fish were leaping that day, someone else certainly was!

Whenever you feel yourself being stifled by **self-limiting rules,** take your freedom back by breaking those rules.

Perhaps the fisherman hadn't thought that what I was doing was silly or childish; perhaps he might even have envied me or wanted to join in himself. But even if he had thought my activity ridiculous, at least I had given him a story to tell and something to think about whilst waiting for the fish to bite. In any event the **burst of activity** on the trampoline, and the laughter that had rocked through me as I imagined what the fisherman might be thinking, certainly served to unblock my mental state that afternoon.

PROMISES JAR

On of the most effective ways to foster creativity is to induce **relaxation**. In fact, it's been medically proven that it is impossible to feel anxious and relaxed at the same time. The two states simply cannot co-exist. It therefore naturally follows that the more relaxed you can become, the less stressed or anxious you will feel. However, for many people finding the time and conditions in which they are able to relax, may not always be easy.

One major problem, especially for working parents, is the idea that **making time** to do something strictly for you is really quite selfish. But, of course, it's just the opposite. The reason for this is that when you're more relaxed and happy, those feelings will also transmit to the rest of the family and, what's more, you will find that you will in fact **have more time and energy** as a result of relaxing for while, than you ever could in your previously stressed or anxious state. In this case self-interest is also self-survival.

So, start **breaking your old self-imposed taboos** and regulations, and give yourself the attention and care you need in order to allow yourself the complete freedom to begin to walk on the grass. And one very creative way in which you could begin to do this is to establish your very own Promises Jar.

It's a very simple idea: Just write down on a large piece of paper, separating each item on the paper with a little space, **a list of activities** that you really enjoy, and that you consider relaxing. You can even add a few that are positively self-indulgent! Your choices don't have to involve great expense, and need not involve any travelling or inconvenience at all. Here are a few ideas to get you started:

- *Have a luxurious bath*
- *Build something, make a model or create something*
- *Paint a picture*
- *Write a poem*
- *Watch a comedy film or Listen to a comedy CD*
- *Play a sport you enjoy*
- *Write a 'have done' list*
- *Treat yourself to a special lunch*
- *Go for a walk in the countryside*
- *Go fishing*

The choices are all yours, but make sure they include activities that really will help you to feel more **relaxed and comfortable**. You could even refer to the list of 32 things to do before you are eleven, which you will find in Chapter 1. Don't restrict yourself either, but **write down as many things as you can think of.** Then, when you have completed your list, cut out each item individually, fold the pieces of paper in half and then in half again, and simply put them in a **clean empty jar.**

Once your jar is in place, the next time you feel you need to take some time out for yourself, just dip your hand into the jar and pull out one of the promises. Remember, you've already **'promised'** yourself that you'll do the named activity, so you'll feel no guilt about it. After all, why should you? It is probably a good idea to tell other family members, or those you may live with, exactly what you intend to do. Who knows, they may think it's an **excellent** idea and start doing it themselves. Even if they don't, they'll respect you more for taking the time to give a little more **well-deserved attention** to yourself. Also make sure that you use your jar at least once a week until it develops into a very good habit indeed.

You can also use your promises jar as a way of rewarding family or friends, and it could make an excellent gift for children to give to their parents. You ask them to write down on a piece of paper fifteen or so activities or chores that they would like you to do for them, and then fold their choices and put them into a different jar. You arrange a time suitable for the activity, and dip into the jar to discover their choice. Not only is it a very **useful way of bonding** with family and friends, but the fun and surprise element is very enjoyable.

WHAT'S IN THE GARDEN SHED THIS TIME?

So far we have examined the importance of **recognising** and **cutting down the patterns** that form your

negative thoughts, and have shown you a variety of methods and means to help you to do this. But, of course, every person is different and unique and will respond according to their own individuality.

In any garden, it is essential to recognise the requirements of the plant you **wish to grow** and flourish; it would be unlikely that you would use the same fertilizer on a potato as you would on a delicate orchid. It is therefore entirely up to you to decide what you yourself need to take from this book in order to advance your own personal development and **achieve the success** you wish for, and so richly deserve. It really doesn't matter which pathway you take, as long as it eventually leads you to finally walking on the grass.

* If you really want to bring about the changes you desire, my recommendation is for you to start using the various tools and techniques you now have at your disposal on a daily basis. You can begin with the simple **Band of Change**, which will help you to cut down on your unhelpful, negative thoughts, and show you how easily you can provide positive replacements. You can also begin to change or break your habits.

✤ Why not make a start by doing something different today? Or perhaps you are already mentally starting to **build your bonfire**, getting ready to burn those planks of dead wood.

✤ Or you may be looking forward to whatever activity you will pluck from your **promises jar**, and anticipating the feeling of relaxation and self-care that will bring much needed balance in your life as you prepare for your walk on the grass.

Chapter 5

Mirror Mirror on the Wall

IMAGINE WHAT YOU COULD LOOK LIKE

Many years ago my seven year old daughter asked her Grandma:
"Nan, in the olden days when you were young, was everything black and white, even the grass?" Her Grandma sat silently and reflective, "No she replied, the grass was still very green"

I was silently amused. Who wouldn't be? Of course, I didn't laugh or in any way hurt my daughter's feelings, because I fully understood how she had come to ask such a question. This was merely a child's perception of a difficult period in history. Everything she had previously seen or read about that time, when her grandmother had been young, had indeed been very grey and dark. And I think it's fair to say that there was no darker period than the era of the Second World War.

Fortunately the war finally ended, and, preceded by the new Technicolor newsreels and Hollywood films, **colour again** came flooding back into everyone's life. Deprived of it for so long, vibrant colours very quickly became the order of the day in the 1950s. It seemed that as richer colour appeared, the more moods were lifted.

The fact is that in times of great difficulty, in times of great stress, the world does indeed become a very grey and dark place. It's a **perception** that we have all probably had at one time or another.

In this chapter the aim is to become more creative with your own image, the part of yourself that you **display** to the outside world. For many people wishing to improve their personal success, image often becomes neglected on the journey to self actualisation. If it appears at all, it is often by accident at the culmination of your success rather than the inception of it. But consider this. When you improve your image the personal impact you make is immediate; people who have previously ignored your very existence begin to **notice** you. More importantly, changing your image is another way to get your creativity really **bubbling**.

A WORLD OF COLOUR

Colour is extremely important for the stimulation of creativity. Creativity, after all, simply means the **actualisation of thoughts** or ideas into realities by the use of intelligence and imagination. It works like this: You focus on an idea or concept in your mind to form a picture. Then, using your imagination, you create a picture so vivid and colourful that the mind is forced into giving it attention. The brighter and more colourful the picture becomes in your mind, the greater the likelihood of it turning into **reality**. I don't claim this as my own discovery: It is a fact supported by any number of reputable publications written on the subject of self development.

The truth is that without colour the world would be a very dull place indeed. And it is the same for the territory of the mind, which thrives on colour. Can you, for one moment, just imagine a world in which everything is black and white? Dreary, isn't it? Fortunately, you don't have to live in that world. You have the **incredible gift of sight**. And here's where we're going to help you use it in order to stimulate your creativity so that you are ready to start really walking on the grass.

LOOKING ON THE BRIGHTSIDE

So, ask yourself now, what is your image portraying to the world, how much colour do you really have in your life? Let's refer to the clothes you choose to wear as a starting point.

> *You can begin by observing what the people around you are wearing now. Are they wearing dull coloured clothes, grey and black perhaps? Or are the colours they are wearing brighter, more noticeable, and vibrant?*

The differences can appear more overt in the winter or summer. Usually summer clothes tend to be much brighter; winter clothing is often far more sombre. Look at what you see people wearing now to validate this point. And yet there really are **no rules** to obey regarding your choice as to what you wear, except your own self-imposed rules. There is absolutely nothing written in any book of etiquette that requires you to be drab in the winter, or **bright in summer**. So why do so many people tend to wear only dark clothes, dull black and grey, in the winter? Surely, it's your choice to wear whatever you want, whenever you want, irrespective of the season. Remember you can Walk on the Grass anytime you choose to.

DRESS IN MONOTONE LIVE A MONOTONE EXISTENCE

Before moving into Psychology, I started out in my career as a Designer. Perhaps this is why **colour** has always been an important part of my life. Having said that, at times colour sometimes left even me behind. I became particularly aware, that during periods when I wasn't enjoying my job or the environment I was working in, that I actually began losing my feel for colour. For some reason I began to dress like everyone around me: I wore plain colours, grey, white or black. Perhaps it was a way of disappearing into the background, becoming invisible in an environment I no longer wanted to remain in. I knew for a fact that my **mood** was low at that time, and that my creativity had well and truly retired to sulk up in the attic.

If this is your state at the moment, then it really is time to **emerge** from **hibernation**. It doesn't matter whether you are male or female, young or old. Perhaps it's high **time for a change**. As you read through the following list of questions, pause for a moment and observe what you can see and what you may be feeling:

> *What are you wearing?* ....
> *Does it make you feel good?* ....
> *Does it inspire you?* ....
> *Does it make you feel like you could take on the world?* ....
> *If you had arranged to meet someone for lunch that really inspired you, would you still choose to wear the same clothes you are wearing now?* ....
> *If the answer to the last question is no, then why not?* ....

I imagine that the penultimate question may have caught you out, because it is so easy to fall into the trap of safety and comfort with what you wear. The fact is that when you are meeting someone whom you really respect and admire, your enthusiasm for an **image change** systematically rises to another level.

With some of you, the answers might be qualified by a few 'If only' reflections, such as:

🌟 Ahh, but I can't because.................

🌟 Ahh, but it's the industry I work in.........................and variations on this theme.

And if you think this is not at all relevant to you, then just consider this: It may be that you really don't want to stand out. However, the fact is that if you really want to **pump up your creativity** and become more inspired then you have to stand out to some degree. Again it's a question of learning to break down the barriers that are keeping you rooted and standing still. You have to find your own **natural image**, the part of yourself that reflects the unique individual that you are. It doesn't have to be too overtly different, but you can at least be the one shiny penny in the jar of old pennies, can't you? You won't be in any way physiologically different, but what will shine through is the **difference** in how you think.

I anticipate hearing some people groaning: "I don't care what I wear; I just get dressed in whatever I want". Well in that case I'd like to refer you back to the chapter **on habits and beliefs**, because it's possible you could well be stuck in a rut. This is relevant to men in particular who may advocate that they have no choice but to wear suits everyday for work and can't get creative but I disagree; the shirt you wear, the tie you wear are all relevant and open to inspiration. To explain what I mean by this, I would like you to ask yourself:-

> *How much of your image is habit?*

What you need to understand is that habits are the ivy of the creative world, not an unpleasant plant to look at, but if you allow it to continue growing unchecked then sooner or later it will strangle your creativity. In order to reach your full creative potential you must first begin by **weeding out the suffocating ivy** of sheer habit. If you don't, it may choke you.

And now, consider what the following message is really saying:" I'm not bothered about what I wear". What impression do you think it gives to other people around you? And what about the message you are giving to yourself: "I'm not bothered about me"?

Your **image is so important**. It's what marks you out as an individual, and allows you to fully express yourself. It is you in the shop window, displayed before the world.

> *Do you really believe that appearances do not matter? How do you yourself tend to notice the people around you? Are you influenced in any way by how they dress? Take a look now, or the next time you are amongst people. And be honest with yourself. Do some people attract you more than others? Do some people repel you more than others? And if so – why?*

But you may still argue: I'm still creative no matter how I may appear to others. The point is that I am not encouraging you to simply be creative. I want you to use **creativity for you personally**. I am inviting you to swim in waters you've barely touched with your toes before, to open your eyes in order that you may really see clearly the wonderful opportunities before you. I want you to experience life as you've never done before, going **beyond the restrictions** of all those old and useless habits that may have been holding you back for so long. I want you to break your own rules and shock yourself with the infinite possibilities that life holds for you.

Now, let's examine another landmark that will be your **guiding light** throughout this creative journey. It is that of self-awareness, which is both an internal and an external experience. However, if this is true, why is it that so much that is written about **self-awareness** is based purely on the internalisation process?

John was a client whom I considered very creative. He was a confident, competent professional. But John was not receiving the recognition he felt his work deserved and was being overlooked, particularly in the promotion stakes. He came to see me at quite a low time. He had learned that he was being made redundant. And, like many of us faced with a similar career crisis, John recognised that he was losing confidence and self esteem. During our discussions it became apparent that deep down John was very secure with his real internal self, and there seemed very little he wished to change. However, it steadily emerged that John was deeply dissatisfied with the external image he believed he portrayed to the rest of the world. So I set him the task set out below. A couple of weeks later John came back to see me, and I could tell that there was a new enthusiasm about him. He seemed totally energised, positively buzzing. He told me how he now had strong images in his mind about who he wanted to be, about the kind of persona he wanted to project onto the world. But the new image he had in mind wasn't a singular image, but rather a collection of images. And the new person he wanted to be was unique. He was no longer, he realised, one dimensional, but had come to find his true self. This revelation restored his confidence, his self esteem, and soon his creative juices were flowing as never before. Shortly afterwards he found a new and much better job, and he's never been happier in his life. And now he is indeed truly walking on the grass.

By the same token you too can release that **creative flow** by changing your own image, ridding yourself of tired old habits, and unhelpful ways of thinking about yourself. And to prove how easily you can do it, I recommend that you too study and follow the exercise below:

If you really do want to **walk on the grass**. Don't be afraid to **change the way you look**. It's nothing to do with spending thousands of pounds on designer clothes. Just follow these few simple techniques, and see how very easy it can be.

LOOKING GOOD – FEELING GOOD

So if you're ready to start to make that change. If you're ready to learn how to dress in order to inspire yourself, we'll begin. Here are some guidelines that really will work for you.

> *If it doesn't make you feel good, then don't wear it!*

Why on earth would you choose to wear something that doesn't add to your **feeling of well-being**? Worse than that, why wear clothing that actually makes you feel drab, dreary and miserable. Well, of course, you wouldn't if you thought about it. And yet if you closely examine the habitual way in which you dress, can you honestly say that you don't ever do this? I mean that you don't ever dress yourself in order to ensure you stay miserable. I know I used to do, and I'll bet most people do at one time or another. It's so easy, isn't it, to simply throw on clothes without even thinking about it, especially when we are in a rush or tell yourself that you are not going out so who will see you. The difference is that now you ARE going to **start thinking about it.** From now on, I'm asking you to start wearing only clothes that **make you feel good** at any time of the day and whoever you are with. I'm asking you to be consciously aware of what you are choosing to wear. The criterion is very simple:

> *Ask yourself this question as you are dressing yourself each morning:*
> **'Does what I've chosen to wear, make me feel really good?'**

If the answer is 'no', then perhaps you should give the clothing to some worthy charity. Certainly do not wear it today or perhaps ever again.

GET TO KNOW WHAT DOES MAKE YOU FEEL GOOD

But where do I start?

This is an age in which we are constantly bombarded with images. Advertisers ensure that there is little respite from it. You may believe that you are not affected by these images, but subconsciously you will automatically be making your own judgements on what you like and what you don't like. Think about these two questions: Do some advertisements appeal to you? Are there other advertisements that really annoy you?

1. To really understand what you genuinely do like, and what it is that makes you feel good, I suggest you **start collecting image ideas** from some of these sources;
   * Magazines
   * Newspapers
   * Hoardings and billboards
   * TV
   * Shop windows
2. Then I suggest that whenever you see an image you really like, even if it is an image on Television, take an instant photograph on your camera phone, presuming that you may have one.

However, if you don't have this facility, try to impress that **image on to your mind** so that you are certain to retain it.

3. The next step is to **print off your photographs**, or cut out the images that appeal to you most from articles or illustrations and collate them together in a scrapbook, folder or album. You may be genuinely surprised at the pattern that emerges; often you'll see similar colours and styles repeating themselves.

There's no need to gain confirmation on whether your choices appeal to others. The **choices are yours**, they are personal and reflective of the real you.

And for those girls who may be reading this, remember that if you have to ask someone else for their opinion of what you are wearing, then you probably have doubts about it yourself already, so it isn't right for you.

> *Remember that famous question "does my bum look big in this?" if you have to ask the question, then it probably does, or at least you think it does. Change the item of clothing or you'll spend all your time thinking negatively about how you look regardless of who has told you differently.*

Each of us knows what it is that we like, what **draws and attracts** us, just as we know the things that repel us. So feel perfectly comfortable with your **choices**. Fixing the image in your mind using photographs or illustrations will make it easier for you to express a real opinion on your choices.

Often I've undertaken this activity with teenagers, always with the same positive results. Teenagers in particular are completely honest in

expressing their opinions of what it is that they like. If you're parent you will understand this, and recall the debates and battles you may have had over what your child should wear. It is sometimes an unfortunate tendency of parents to override or discount their children's own preference of what to wear; so much so that the children become confused themselves as to what really suits them. Allowing them to have a **greater say in their choice** of clothing, when it's reasonable for them do so, can be very **empowering** for a child and can also lift a child's confidence dramatically. The following example may help to explain this:

> *Emma was a young girl who changed literally overnight, transformed from a disillusioned, grungy teenager into the real person she wanted to be. She followed the suggestion of collecting images that appealed to her, and very soon realised that she was no longer the tom boy she had represented as a toddler. When she finally realised she had a choice of finding her own real self, of expressing her own real image to the outside world, her confidence increased immeasurably, and her creativity became inspired.*

Over time, many of us become conditioned to the expectations others have of us. Taken to the extreme this acting out of life so as not to alarm others or **change their expectation** of us equates to being imprisoned in a closed box, with no clear way out. We find that we are unable to think for ourselves, or to express ourselves clearly. We become stifled, and so does our creativity. It is imperative therefore that we find our own **true image**, our own true selves.

UNDERSTANDING COLOUR

There is no simpler way of acquainting yourself with the **colours that appeal to you** than visiting the local hardware or DIY store and searching out paint samples. So as a first step to emerging from grey hibernation:

1. Visit a Hardware store or Do it Yourself store
2. Find the **paint** mixing section
3. In this area you are likely to find a range of **sampler** cards with varying colour shades, which are generally free to take away. They are also available on the internet now as well.
4. Spend a few minutes really examining the **colour** ranges in relation to your image.
5. Consider carefully which colours you are most **drawn** to. Notice the colours and shades that inspire you that seem to energise you and generally make you feel good.
6. You may be attracted to several different colours or shades, Take away all the colour cards that you like and **label them** A, B or C as follows.
   - ❋ A - these colours makes you **feel good** – you could immerse yourself in these colours
   - ❋ B - these colour shades **appeal to you**, although you wouldn't dress yourself in them from head to foot
   - ❋ C - colours that you **like elements of**– and may wear with accessories such as a belt, a tie, etc
7. The final step is to go home and **re-organise** your wardrobe, ensuring that you're consciously aware of how many items you have already in your best colour A. These are the items of clothing that are likely to make you feel much more creative and confident.

In seven easy steps you will reduce the size of your wardrobe, increase your creative thinking, feel more **confident** and improve your image all at the same time.

TIME TO TAKE STOCK

And, of course, your image is not all about clothes or the way you dress. You can carry out these **simple steps** on virtually every area of your life. Discover what you really like to eat; what colour car you prefer to drive, the colour or colours you choose to decorate your home. You will realise very quickly whether you are becoming really **inspirational** with your creativity, or whether you are surrounding yourself with colours that only neutralise your enthusiasm for change. Take a **real inventory** of your life, appraising fully any areas which seem to be holding you back. Allow colour and image to help you to **break through**, even change the colour of the pen you write with. Here's another example of the way change can come about so easily:

> *Sarah was a work colleague who approached me because of a weight problem she had for many years. As with many overweight people, Sarah was constantly trying new and ever more complex diets, all of which failed miserably. It struck me quite early on that inspiration was markedly lacking in Sarah, and had been absent in her for some time. She was very despondent and low in mood. Inevitably we talked about LOSING weight. I wanted to turn the statement on its head, so I asked her when was the last time that she had enjoyed losing something. I was pointing out to her that generally the word 'losing' simply brings back memories of never finding something you've lost. In short, the word itself has very negative connotations.*

I also asked Sarah to tell me how she **visualised** herself whenever she imagined herself reaching her ideal weight. Without hesitation she immediately referred to a picture of herself as she had been as a 16-year-old. I said that unfortunately there was no time machine in existence that could take her back to being 16 again. However, I suggested, she could easily reclaim some of those creative skills she had possessed when she was 16, and start to use them to help her now. Directing her to use the **Looking Good Feeling Good** - exercises already set out regarding the making of choices, I encouraged her to focus on her future and not on past events that were already gone and could never be recalled. I suggested she should direct her creativity, her imagination, not on the self she perceived herself to be now, but on the self **she wanted to be in the future**. You see, nothing can change unless we are prepared to let go of the past. Sure enough, within a couple of weeks she came back to see me, totally positive with the **new images** she had created and enthused with inspiration of who she wanted to be. And without really thinking about it directly, she had defined her ultimate goal.

As most people may testify, reducing your weight substantially is no mean feat. It takes commitment, perseverance and self-belief, and more than a little inspiration. Sarah had used the **power of self-imaging** to achieve all these components for real change. Twelve months later, a stunning blonde lady stood before me. She still had her image file in her hand, and had added to it considerably. And what a **transformation**: Sarah had actually become exactly what she wanted to be. She now felt empowered, and was oozing enthusiasm with her newly transformed image.

Everyone can make these subtle changes. And once achieved they remain like immoveable anchors to bring inspiration into your life naturally.

IMAGINE WHAT'S IN THE GARDEN SHED NOW

In this chapter we've considered the dramatic way in which a change of image can **enhance your personal success**.

Everyone has the ability to instantly carve the way in which they are perceived by other people.

* You simply need to cut out some old ways of thinking and break a few of your own self-imposed rules, because it will be of no surprise to you that if you **look good, you'll feel good.** And if you feel good, you will automatically begin to think more positively.
* We've also looked at what **dressing consciously** really means, and how important it is to portray yourself to your best advantage to the world. Who would have thought a trip to the local hardware store would really bring so many colours back into your life? And it needn't stop there; you can change your outlook on every aspect of life.
* Try new things, enliven your mind with variety, whether it's visiting a **new restaurant**, a different supermarket, or even finding

a new and alternative route to work. The more you open yourself to change, the more your life will be refreshed with a new vibrancy.

* Dress every day in readiness of meeting the **person that inspires** you most, and soon you'll find that you are being inspired by yourself.

These subtle changes can be introduced easily, and will eventually act like anchors to bring creativity into your life naturally.

WALK ON THE GRASS

Chapter 6

She Shoots She Scores

ENHANCED GOAL SETTING

The atmosphere was incredibly tense. Everyone present was on the edge of their seat, shuffling nervously. You could feel the anticipation in the air. All the adults were rapt, incredulous at the prospect of a dream come true. You could almost smell the freshness of the grass though the TV screen. Already, to have come this far seemed almost too good to be true. Suddenly goals were coming thick and fast. Each time the ball found the back of the net, the group would leap to their feet as one and begin shouting and shrieking. At last the final whistle blew, and the room erupted in celebration. Even as a four year old, I could feel the electric atmosphere and knew something very significant had just occurred. Sitting within the warmth of my family, I had my first experience of what it felt like to achieve a true 'goal'. The event, of course, was the 1966 World Cup final, the first ever won by the England football team.

There was no doubt that the England team were inspired on that day, back in 1966. And it's that same kind of inspiration that you will need in order to achieve your own personal goals. Only when you can feel that unique and **powerful explosion of enthusiasm** can you really know that you've succeeded. It's a truly wonderful and energising feeling, but the process of success must first begin with the identification of your real 'goal', characterised by a special desire to succeed that you feel deep inside your mind.

But goals may not always be what they seem. In fact, it's quite usual to confuse real goals with the various steps or tasks that lead us towards their **achievement**. I have had many discussions with people who have similarly confused a goal list for what was in reality a list of tasks associated with achieving that **main goal**. Of course, any step aimed at self improvement is never a bad thing and proves that, at least, you are moving in the right direction. But it is really important to identify your real goals if you are determined to achieve them. The associated tasks can greatly assist you, but they are invariably composed of the **small pieces** that fit together to complete the picture, and are not the full picture in themselves.

Sometimes it can take a great many pieces fitting together, as with a jigsaw, to complete your **success pictur**e. And while each piece of the **jigsaw** has its role to play, the pieces must be put together in the correct order in order to achieve the desired outcome. Would you, for example, throw all the pieces of a jigsaw on the floor and expect them to fit together perfectly to complete your picture? I don't think so.  Unfortunately that can be the expectation when people have an end goal in mind, but haven't **properly formulated** the steps they need to take, before the goal can be achieved.

Let me give you an example of this type of thinking, one that I've come across many times. It can be typified in the way that some people view early retirement. Often people in this position consider the advantages of taking up this option, and will enthusiastically discuss all the things they will be able to do when they actually retire. And although the list of **activities** they **enthuse over** is usually very comprehensive, and includes genuine interests, they make no actual plan for when or how they will begin to undertake these activities once the early retirement looms.

In fact a very large percentage of this group will wait until the day they actually retire before throwing the jigsaw pieces on the floor, expecting them to form the **perfect picture of their future**. Unfortunately they are usually disappointed when the pieces still remain mixed up and unconnected. After the novelty of the first few weeks of no longer working, many begin to find themselves at a loss, wondering what to do with all this additional free time.

Quite soon, some begin to heartily regret the decision: They realise, in many cases, that they have exchanged a busy and **productive working life**, surrounded by colleagues and friends, for a permanent state of wondering what to do next. Quite often by this stage, if they are with a partner, one or other of them will be slowly climbing the walls as the frustration bred of inactivity and the constant proximity of the loved one slowly becomes unbearable. Eventually many of these early retired people find themselves in a rut of perpetual mind-numbing boredom, and **new** negative **habits** surrounding their inactivity begin to take root.

They may find that they are sleeping longer, simply for the want of something meaningful to do, or eating more and exercising less. And because they may be still fairly young and physically and financially comfortable, these new habits become ever more difficult to break or to change once they have become **established**. Unfortunately for many of them, they made the mistake of thinking that the goal was to take early retirement: It might have been better if they had looked beyond it and considered exactly what they were going to do once that retirement had taken place. But it's never too late to make sure that your own future is likely to be far more fulfilling; perhaps all you need is a **Croak list**.

BUILDING YOUR CROAK LIST

> *"Daddy, can you make a noise like a frog," little Ben asked his father. "No," replied his Dad, curiously, "why do you ask?" "Well" said Ben, disappointed, "Mummy said that when you croak it, we are all off to Acapulco."*

You have probably heard the terms 'bucket list' or 'top 101 things to do before you die'. There was a recent successful film, starring Morgan Freeman and Jack Nicholson, which depicted the two very different characters, both suffering from terminal cancer, fulfilling a common desire to spend the time they have left doing everything they ever wanted to do before they "kick the bucket". Now, I'm not suggesting that you are likely to "kick the bucket" any time soon, but it occurs to me that we shouldn't wait until death threatens before we get around to doing **everything we really want to do**. In fact I see no reason why we can't start doing these things right now?

It's a fairly simple process to begin compiling your own **Croak List,** or, in other words, a list of everything you ever wanted to do before you die. Perhaps you might prefer to do it in collaboration with a partner, or even include the whole family. I call it the Croak list, simply because I love the frog joke, but you can call it whatever you wish. It's irrelevant **how many activities** you put on your Croak List, but I am recommending that you aim for at least one hundred. Not only will it be a **pleasurable exercise** to think of things you would really love to do, but it gives a partnership a joint focus on the future, and once the ideas are **planted in your mind**, your creativity will be encouraged into finding ways and means of achieving completion of the items on your list.

GETTING STARTED WITH YOUR 'CROAK LIST'

In order to get you started on **constructing your list**, I've compiled a few questions to inspire your thinking along the right lines. Don't be concerned if it takes a little while for your creativity to take over so that your list begins to flow, that's perfectly natural.

> *What would put a smile on your face?*
> *What experiences do you want to have?*
> *What do you want to achieve at work or home?*
> *Who would you like to help?*
> *What change would make a huge difference to your life?*
> *Where would you like to visit?*
> *What would you like to own?*

Once you've listed your top **one hundred goals** on your Croak list, make a pact with yourself or if it's a joint one, with your partner, that you'll achieve at least three or more of your goals every year. Review the list completely and regularly to check your progress. It may be that some of the top 10 items that **inspired you originally** may not be as appealing as they once were, whereas those that were listed lower now seem far more attractive. This is simply your creative mind taking over, making you aware of other features regarding your **choices** that perhaps you hadn't previously considered. But remember, the choices are entirely yours, as are the rules for selecting them.

You can download a list of over a hundred ideas from my website at www.angelawhitlock.com.

1	2	3	4	5
6	7	8	9	10
11	12	13	14	15
16	17	18	19	20
21	22	23	24	25
26	27	28	29	30
31	32	33	34	35
36	37	38	39	40
41	42	43	44	45
46	47	48	49	50
51	52	53	54	55
56	57	58	59	60
61	62	63	64	65
66	67	68	69	70
71	72	73	74	75
76	77	78	79	80
81	82	83	84	85
86	87	88	89	90
91	92	93	94	95
96	97	98	99	100

When you have completed your list, **focus on the top three items**, the Croak goals you would most love to achieve within the next 12 months. As you do this you will begin to notice how you really feel about them. For instance, does thinking about them bring a smile to your face? Once you have achieved your goals, will you feel as though you have won your **own personal World Cup**? If simply thinking about them causes you to feel excited and enthusiastic, then you've probably chosen very well.

INSPIRED INTO ACTION

Again, considering your top three goals on a scale of 0 to 100, what is your temperature gauge indicating? Is your thermostat of enthusiasm pointing towards 80 percent, or is it lower? If it is indicating lower than 80 percent, then I suggest you may need to **examine your motivation** a little more closely before we move on. To help you to do this, consider each of the top three goals one at a time and answer the following questions:

> *Will achieving the goal really excite you?*
> *Will it add to the quality of your life?*
> *Is it creative?*
> *Does it scare you?*
> *What would be different in your life if you achieved this goal?*
> *What would be the consequences in your life if you didn't achieve this goal?*

Sometimes it can clarify things to focus on what life would be like if you didn't achieve that particular goal; the usual conclusion is that life would remain pretty much as it is and therefore the consequences are likely to be quite minor. If this is the case then your motivation could easily wane under pressure. However, the implications of **actually achieving the goal** could be very much greater, and could indeed possibly be life-changing. This **realisation** in itself could provide some of the motivation you require in order to achieve that goal.

Amongst the goals on my own personal Croak list, I have included at least one activity each year that really **scares me**. Obviously different things scare different people, and I really don't advocate that you take up any activity that may be life-threatening or foolhardy. However, I find that

facing up to our fears, if only in a small way, is very good preparation for meeting other challenges we may have to confront in life. Overcoming the fear can also instil greater self-confidence, as well as getting your **pulse racing** and **adrenalin flowing** to make you feel really alive. Feel free to be as creative as you possibly can with your goals, for example a simple goal to 'Visit Mexico' could be transformed into; 'Visit Mexico and wear sombreros' like the three amigos'. Add creativity and fun to all your goals whether they are work or home related and you'll think differently and will be more likely to achieve them.

SABOTAGING THE CROPS

If you have already been unsuccessful in achieving any of the goals on your list when it was previously attempted in the past, it could be due to factors of which you were not consciously aware.

Ask yourself the following:

> *If you achieve your goal are you ready for the consequences?*

It's not unusual for people to sabotage their own efforts of achieving goals, though the sabotage is usually very subtle and performed **unconsciously**. Often it is borne out of the fear that success might change your life too radically, and that you would be forced into making decisions that you weren't yet ready to make.

Being more aware of the possibility of this happening will help you to overcome it. There should really be no need to hide from any consequences of **achieving your goal**. But if you really feel that you're not yet ready to achieve a particular goal, then simply change your goal to another one that will be more **attainable** and manageable at this time. You can always **upgrade** your goal when you feel ready because you're in control.

TO TRY IS TO FAIL

One major obstacle to achieving personal success may be the actual fear of success itself. One sure way to test whether you are prone to this fear is to examine the language you used when setting the goal. If, for example, you have stressed the word 'try', then it's possible you were setting yourself up for a fall.

This is because the **definition** of the word 'try', actually translates as:

- to endeavour
- to make an effort
- to struggle

All that endeavour, effort and struggle makes success seem like very hard work indeed, doesn't it? You're more likely to form an image of someone working on a chain-gang than the **confident and happy-looking self** you desire to be. If you're ever tempted to say or even think that you'll try something again, just beware that you may be setting yourself up for not achieving simply because you are only 'attempting' to reach a goal.

More often than not when we hear that people have tried to do something, it generally means that they didn't succeed, unless the sentence is completed with a **positive outcome**. By changing your use of vocabulary from 'I'll try' to 'I will', you'll also be changing your thought patterns from negative to positive. You will be surprised at the difference it can make to your goal achievements.

GOALS WITH MODALITIES

People learn in different ways, according to their own cognitive strengths. Whilst some are more adept at **learning visually**, others may favour **listening** (auditory) or practical **hands-on** methods of learning (kinaesthetic). It is therefore very important that you find out what is the best way for you to learn. If you have heightened visual and/or strong audio perception, ensure that you incorporate these modalities as part of your **goal setting techniques**, using the kind of material and imagery that combines these forms. Tapping into your most **perceptive modality** will greatly enhance your possibilities for success in achieving your goals.

In particular, strong visualisation has been proven to be extremely **successful** in helping people to achieve their goals. The bigger, brighter and more vivid the image you project as a **visualisation** of your goal, the more powerful and creative your thoughts will be in directing your mind towards achieving its success.

> *What exactly does your goal look like? Could you create your desired outcome by drawing or illustrating it? It's easier than you think. Remember you can use stick people or shapes for objects; you don't need to be artistic.*
>
> *What does it feel like? – Which words most aptly describe how you will actually feel when your goal is achieved?*
>
> *What does it sound like? Imagine a sound commensurate with achieving success.*

> *In whom could you confide your desire to achieve this goal? How are they likely to respond?*

Once you are able to represent your goal in terms of what it would look like, what it would sound like and how you will feel when you achieve it, the mind can really begin to get very creative towards its actualisation. Here are some ideas to get you started to really bring your goals to life.

A PICTURE PAINTS A THOUSAND WORDS

In order to intensify the process of goal achievement, if you are a visual person then it's recommended that you first create a clear image in your mind of how you imagine your goal will look. You then bring that image to life by having it physically reproduced and displayed before you. Apart from original drawings, illustrations and photographs, it's also possible to have a picture or photograph printed on to a mug or mouse mat, which you can keep in full view on your desk or work station.

With the availability of new technology, this process can be done very cheaply nowadays; certain advertising outlets may even do it for the price of the postage if they think it is likely that you will buy more items from them. The point is this: the more prominently you place that vivid image representation of your goal in your visual view, the more likely and the more quickly you will be able to successfully achieve it.

BUILDING THE JIGSAW

Another visual and kinaesthetic technique to get your creative juices really flowing is to create a **jigsaw of your goal**. You can cut out a picture or illustration from a book or magazine, draw or paint your own picture or take and retain a photograph that closely represents your goal. You then **transform your picture into a jigsaw**. There is a plentiful supply of new technology available, on the internet and in most Photo Shops, that will also enable you to do this very easily and without great expense.

Once your jigsaw has been broken up into parts, you can keep it where it can be regularly viewed. And then each time you feel that an integral part of your goal has been achieved, you simply slot in the relevant part of the jigsaw, perhaps starting with the corners and edges. To reinforce the fact that you are making progress, you can make a **note on the back** of the piece as you join it to the rest of your jigsaw, noting the date and any specific comment you wish to make regarding the achievement of this particular part of your goal. It can be incredibly inspiring to see how you are **moving towards full achievement** of your goal, piece by piece.

COMPUTER PASSWORD

We've touched on this in an earlier chapter, but just to remind you that from a kinaesthetic point of view changing your computer **access password** or e-mail password to something very positive can be rewarding, and related to the achievement of your goal, can be a very effective way of keeping your mind's **attention** centred on attaining your goal.

MOBILE PHONES

From an auditory perspective, you can also change the ring tone of your mobile phone, or even your landline, to sounds or **tunes** directly related to your goals. Your mind will then be reminded of the goal each time the phone rings, thereby reinforcing your desire for success.

Adding **positive words** or phrases to the names in your mobile phonebook as we discussed in earlier chapters is another excellent way of providing added inspiration. For example, Jenny becomes 'Jenny - You did it!' You may be surprised at how such an apparently simple change can substantially increase your positive thought patterns.

GIVING TIME TO YOUR DREAMS

As with the slotting together of a jigsaw, it takes many small component parts to build towards success. It is therefore very important that you **give a time frame** to the achievement of your goals.

If, for instance, you began **taking the first steps today**, and nothing stood in your way, how much time do you think it would take to achieve your goal? When you have arrived at a reasonable estimate, just to be on the safe side and as a contingency against unforeseen circumstances, double that amount of time. You don't want to put yourself under unnecessary pressure before you even begin. This final figure can then serve as an approximation of how long it should take in order to achieve your goal.

You can then follow this **timeline**, keeping a daily plan of your progress. Perhaps you could use the jigsaw example as a means of doing this. It is, of course, entirely up to you how you monitor your own progress, but it is very important that you do so in order to **maintain creative momentum**. It is also a good idea to review your goal on a weekly basis, noting what has been achieved, and ensuring that you are still on track. The more you do this the more the picture of your completed goal will formulate in your mind, and the closer you will be to realising it.

As you establish the habit of **monitoring progress** towards achieving your goal, you will notice increased motivation and a gathering momentum of creative goal-based activity. This is because you are pushing the project to the very forefront of your mind and demanding that it be given maximum attention.

As a final checklist for your goals ensure they follow the CREATE guideline, make them Creative, Realistic, Exciting, Achievable, Timed, and all have an End Outcome.

IS NOURISHMENT IN THE GARDEN SHED NOW?

We nearly have a full set of tools in the Garden Shed now. In this chapter we've examined methods to uncover your real aspirations and desires and how to feed creativity into them to bring them to life.

* Perhaps you've already created your **'Croak List'**, and hopefully had fun doing it. If nothing else, you have at least reminded yourself that there are so many enjoyable and interesting things still waiting for you during your journey through life and it is so inspiring to involve your family and friends.

* We've also looked at the advantages of using different **learning modalities** to enhance your goal scoring capabilities, as well as recommending that you add at least one scary goal a year to the list in order to get your blood circulating, adrenalin pumping, and self-confidence brimming.

* If you struggle to think of a goal that **scares you,** then I suggest you have some fun and go along to a Toastmasters International meeting and join in with the impromptu speaking www.toastmasters.org. Apparently many people quote public speaking as one of the top four most frightening experiences,

along with death but in reality it needn't be and would be a fabulous goal to aim for. A real walk on the grass!

✹ And remember to bring your goals to life, use your mobile phone more effectively, build your goal picture; break it down into **jigsaw pieces** and watch the picture grow as you put it together, monitoring your progress every week until your picture becomes complete.

Let's make the score three nil by the end of the year, as you bang home your first three major goals.

WALK ON THE GRASS

Chapter 7

*It's Not Always What You Know
But Who You Know*

GETTING TO KNOW YOUR SUCCESS TEAM

Before discussing the composition of your own success team, it will be interesting to discover how well you actually know YOU. It may not be easy for you to accept this as a bold statement, but the fact is that the most important person in your life at this present time is YOU. It's not your children, or your family or friends or boss. It is YOU.

Let me explain the reasoning that leads me to this conclusion: Some time ago I was privileged to be employed by the British Red Cross. As you can imagine, I found the work very **interesting**, and felt very proud to be associated with such a greatly respected organisation, which, I believed, existed purely to help others. I was somewhat taken aback, therefore, to discover that the very first thing the Red Cross taught all of their students was the importance of **looking after your own safety**, even before considering the safety of those who might be in desperate straits and seeking immediate aid.

The premise for this was that you could not possibly help anyone else, if you yourself might be in danger or if your involvement in any attempt at rescue or resuscitation might put two people at risk, rather than one. Although, I admit now, this outlook greatly surprised me at first, I gradually came to **clearly see the reason** and logic behind it. Of course in a real life or death situation, none of us can really know how we will respond, and what we will do at the time. But the fact remains that if we are put in situations of harm or danger ourselves, then we can do absolutely nothing to help anyone else that might be in the same predicament.

Another lesson I learned thoroughly, although this lesson took a greater part of my own lifetime to learn, was that If you spend all your **time** and **energy** attempting to make everyone around you happy, not only will you not succeed, but you will never be happy or successful yourself. This is because **happiness** is part of the **journey** towards success. So let's now focus on putting the most important person in your life first. And yes, I'm afraid it's **YOU**.

WHO IS BEHIND THE MASK?

Ursula spent several years learning to drive, but every time she took her test she failed. After so many lessons she had become a very competent driver, so no-one could really understand why she failed so often. Then, during our second meeting, I asked the question: "What was the last examination you failed, I mean, apart from the driving test?" Immediately she was taken back to being 16 again, and the clear recollection of failing an important English examination. Ursula remembered, in particular, the angry response of her mother, who was very upset because she was excellent at English. When we examined the experience together, it became evident that from that day onwards Ursula wore a subconscious mask of failure each time she took a test or examination, ensuring that she would always fail. The label she had chosen to take from her mother had fixed itself so firmly to her mind, that she couldn't rid herself of it.

From the day we are born, we are given a **label**, and have little choice as to whether we really want that label or not. Our first roles on the stage of life are already marked out for us: We are destined to play either a son or daughter, or a brother or sister. As we grow, further and more complex roles are added to our collection. Later on in this chapter, I have compiled a list of what I consider to be the seven main roles that we are all **expected to play**, though I know there are many more. But as each role develops and grows, and our stage-craft becomes more adept, so we also learn to wear a mask. This is because we need to ensure that we are playing the right role at the right time. This mask becomes the face we eventually show to the outside world, the **face we want the rest of the world to see.**

As we grow older and supposedly wiser, it becomes much easier to hide behind the mask, and assume the persona of who we think people want us to be, **subconsciously** conforming to that image. Ursula had taken on the mask of failure because her subconscious mind, wrongly as it turned out, believed it was what her mother expected from her. And her subconscious mind wasn't about to disappoint her mother. It was one of those **classical seeding events** that we mentioned in earlier chapters, with the worst of possible consequences for Ursula. If, instead of responding angrily and referring to her daughter as a failure, Ursula's mother had been sympathetic and **encouraging for the future**, she could have ensured a much brighter outlook for her daughter, which is no doubt what she herself had really wanted. However, once Ursula fully realised that it was someone else's mask she was wearing, and not her own, she decided to remove it. She would never wear it again. Shortly afterwards Ursula took the test once more, and passed with **flying colours.**

Just as we can always be exceptionally creative when we are looking for excuses for not doing anything, we can also apply those same creative abilities to find new disguises whenever we put on our masks. I'll explain what I mean: **Imagine** hiding **behind a tree**. All your body is hidden, and your head is just showing a centimetre at a time. In this way you are able to show just enough of yourself to reveal your physical identity, but nothing else. You are ensuring that you keep the details of your real self to yourself, completely hidden. No-one else will ever get to see who you really are.

Perhaps you may feel it's much safer to hide a large part of yourself from everyone else? However, if you really want to start to **Walk on the Grass** you will need to reveal more than just one glimpse of yourself at a time. You will have to be completely honest with yourself, and allow everyone to know **exactly who you really are**. Life is not a play in which the acting stops when the director shouts 'cut' because the leading actor is playing out of character. Life is about being who you really are, about **being true to yourself**. And, most important of all, the process of life is about developing into the real **authentic** you.

And now it's time to **scare yourself**, but in a good way of course. It's time for you to recognise who really is behind your mask, and what you are showing to the world. But first, let's begin to identify your roles in life:

1. Daughter/son
2. Sister/brother
3. Friend
4. Employee/employer
5. Colleague
6. Husband/wife/partner
7. Father/mother

Taking your role as a daughter or son as a starting point, consider the following questions:

> *When you think about the mask you wear in relation to this role how do you really feel inside?*
> *What do you show to others externally? What do you think they see?*
> *Identify the words which most accurately describe how you honestly and truly think and feel in each of the seven roles, and write them over the faces of each jigsaw puzzle piece.*

Inside Your Mask   **Outside Your Mask**

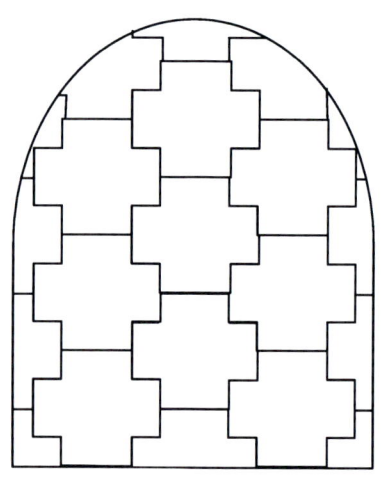

These blank masks are available on the website at
www.angelawhitlock.com

Once you have completed this exercise, you should have a much **greater awareness** of what is actually going on inside your mind, and what you may have to work on in order to improve in the future. The exercise will also point out obstacles which may be barring your success, and will help you to see the **terrain ahead** more clearly so that you can consider and focus on the support you are going to need in order to help you on your way.

We do, of course, have masks for every occasion. Unfortunately, it's the masks that create limiting self-imposed rules that tend to keep us so firmly chained to exactly the same rooted spot.

YOUR SUCCESS TEAM

Continuing on from the previous chapter, by now you have your goals in mind so who can help you to achieve them?

It's very simple in this electronic day and age to keep a list of all your contacts by using your mobile phone or other phone number storage system. This next exercise involves the **compilation of a list of all the people** with whom you have regular contact, both privately and professionally. The object is to then identify those individuals who will either help or hinder you, by putting an **appropriate tick** against their name. Later, in the Brain Drain section which appears further on in this chapter, we'll discuss ways of addressing the people who actually hinder you. In the first stage of the exercise, however, we are concentrating solely on those people you find **positively helpful**.

Here is a typical Help/Hindrance list that you can use and is available on the website at www.angelawhitlock.com:

HELP OR HINDER

Name	Help	Hinder
Person 1		
Person 2		
Person 3		
Person 4		

When you have identified the people who you think are a help to you, go on to consider the attributes they possess by **completing the tick** list below.

Name	Are they Fun?	Are they Creative?	Do they make you feel good?	Do they benefit you in some way?	Do they add to the quality of your life?
Person 1					
Person 2					

It's likely that your **success team** will come from various sources, but the two key groups can be identified as family or friends. The people that you have identified who you really need to concentrate on with help for your goal achievement will materialise in the Creative Column.

FAMILY

When considering the goals you wish to achieve, which family members are most likely to be **helpful to you** in achieving them? If there are family members identified by a tick in the creative box, approach them first to **discuss your aims**, as it is most likely they will provide the greatest amount of help and support to inspire you to success.

FRIENDS

It's likely that you will make many friends over your lifetime, adding to them continuously, whom you can **consider** as part of your success team. Some may come in and out of your life periodically, some may maintain short-term friendships, and others will remain life-time friends. But it really doesn't matter what particular role they play, they will all make some contribution towards your **achievement** of personal success.

SHORT TIME FRIENDS

Short time friends are those people you may meet for a specific purpose. They may only be in your life for a very short time, but they will nevertheless meet a need by **helping and supporting** you, both mentally and physically during that period of time. It's almost as though they come into your life to fulfil a purpose, only to quickly leave it again when that purpose has been achieved. Short term friends may include people you have met on holiday. Perhaps you or they intended to keep in touch, but for some reason you never did. They simply entered your life for a short time, and then quickly drifted out of it again. But for the limited time it lasted, your acquaintance was very **enjoyable**, and the memory of it will remain with you. To use an analogy, your short-time friendship could represent a **Poppy**, a lovely flower which appears briefly in the spring and then simply disappears when the season ends.

SHORT TERM FRIENDS

Short term friendships will last for longer. Inevitably you will spend more time with short term friends, sharing, developing and learning from each other. A short term friend could be a neighbour, a work colleague or could be someone you met at a business or social gathering. You remain friends as long as you are both in the same proximity. However, once either of you moves out of that particular environment, the friendship also tends to drift away. But you will retain **pleasant memories** of your short term friends, possibly for the rest of your life, as well as the **knowledge and learning** you have gained from them. Often both parties would wish the friendship to continue, but the effort it takes to do this is sometimes not sufficient to create the momentum required to keep the friendship strong. The analogy for short term friendship would be similar to the one used to describe a short time friendship: A **daffodil** emerges, flourishes brightly for a few short weeks and then gradually returns back into the earth.

LIFE TIME FRIENDS

It's estimated that, across the wider population, most people will have between three and five long term friends. If you have more, then you can count yourself very fortunate. Life time friends, as the phrase suggests, grow up together, **constantly learn from and support each other**, with both parties making a concerted effort to keep the friendship very much alive. They are the friends you turn to first in a crisis, and they in turn will look for your **support** in similar circumstances. They are the friends you can always count on and are there for you whenever you need them the most.

Life time friends are also the people with whom you want to **spend most of your time**, although dependent on geography and circumstances, it may not always be possible. They are the ones whose **opinions and advice you value the most**. Lifetime friends are perennials, hardy shrubs that flourish through all the seasons, including the harshest winters.

But whatever level your friendships are at, guard them well because they are one of your greatest and **most useful assets in life**. If you really want to start to **walk on the grass**, pay the closest attention to developing all of your friendships, tending them and cherishing them as much as you possibly can. As human beings we all need to be part of a group, a collective. It's in our very nature to have a sense of belonging. We simply cannot exist satisfactorily entirely on our own, nor should we want to. So, make the effort to develop your own circle of friends, and make it as wide as possible. In this very modern age there really are so many ways to keep in touch with long distance friends, from the mobile phone and camera to social networking, as well as through e-mail and easily accessible internet sites. The larger the group of friends you have the more access you have to invaluable skills and knowledge that may just be the help you need and the **greater your success team** will be. But, more importantly, the more balanced your life will feel.

ROLES AND RESPONSIBILITIES OF YOUR SUCCESS TEAM

Once you have gathered your list of people, your success team, and identified the way in which they can actually support you, you can apply their various attributes to the RACI matrix below in relation to your list of goals. RACI simply stands for **responsible, accountable, consult and inform**

RACI is utilised as a model for assigning roles and responsibilities:

Responsibility - People who are expected to actively **participate** in the goal and contribute towards its achievement by using the best of their abilities.

Accountability - The person who is ultimately **responsible** for the results.

Consultation- People who have a particular **expertise** and can **contribute** to specific decisions.

Inform - People who are **affected** by the activity/decision and therefore need to be kept informed, but do not participate in the effort. An important aspect of their role is to keep other similarly affected parties also informed of progress.

RACI MATRIX

Goal	Person 1 - YOU	Person 2	Person 3	Person 4
Goal 1	A	R	C	
Goal 2	A	C		

It may be that one individual could have more than one role, but the matrix will accurately focus your mind on who is able to help you and how they may do it.

The next step is to **ask them for help** for whichever area of support you need. One of the many reasons that we don't receive help is because we haven't asked, perhaps for fear of rejection or embarrassment. But remember the **risk** and reality **chapter**, what have you really got to lose; if we ask but only receive a rejection, then simply ask someone else. You cannot possibly know whether someone will help you unless you ask them, but always assume the **answer is yes** until you hear otherwise.

STANDING DOWN THE BRAIN DRAIN TEAM

Jo had an older sister who, whenever they met up, constantly undermined her. As a result of this, throughout her life Jo always felt like the uneducated younger child of the family, no matter how successful she may have become. When in conversation with Jo, I touched on the subject of the control she felt her sister had over her. Jo responded uncomfortably, admitting that although she believed she loved her sister, she didn't actually like her as a person. In fact, Jo described her sister as very controlling and unpleasant, adding that any help or assistance she ever gave always came with a cost attached to it. Jo also admitted to feelings of regret, adding that her sister had not always been like that; in fact Jo still had some lovely memories of the fun and joy they had shared together when they were both younger. It saddened Jo to realise that all that was gone now.

In order to help Jo to let go of these sad and painful memories of the past, and so be able to move on, she **undertook** the following three activities, which I recommended:

1. She **forgave** her sister for how she had previously treated her

2. She **changed the name** she would use when referring to her older sister – Jo had always called her sister by her nickname Jules. She decided that from now on she would call her sister by her full name, Juliette. In doing this, Jo felt able to **separate her memories** of the young girl, with whom she had once had fun, from the bitter woman she felt her sister had now become. Strangely enough, the older sister didn't even notice the changed form in which Jo now began addressing her.

3. She **stopped all contact** with her older sister, apart from attending unavoidable social occasions.

I suspect that we have all had experience of people who drain us, both mentally and physically. They have the power to literally drain us of energy and optimism, much in the way that a Leech supposedly drains blood from its victims. And yet despite this, for some reason we keep these people in our lives, continuing sometimes, very long-term friendships with them. But why on earth do we, when we have a choice?

It is likely that your reaction to contact with these people may follow a familiar and all too disheartening pattern: The phone rings and the minute you hear that familiar voice your heart sinks because you know that, whatever you are about to hear, it is most unlikely to be good news. Is this beginning to sound familiar yet? Generally members of the **Brain Drain club** are likely to conform to the 'what if' or the 'ahh but' school of attitudes, as we discussed in earlier chapters. Far from supporting you, in reality this type of person will drain you of both **energy and positivity**.

Unfortunately some Brain Drain members may be closer than you would wish, as members of your own family. But even if you are related you haven't signed a contract insisting that you must 'like' them. Neither do family ties commit you to **engaging with them** for the rest of your life. As with all friendships, you have the choice of continuing to allow them to invade your personal territory, of being harangued by their perpetual problems and negativity, and of listening to their whinging and whining whenever nothing ever seems to go right for them. Or you can choose to distance yourself from it all, and from them. Of course it's never easy to break off **communication** with other family members, particularly when those guilty feelings creep up on you, whispering in your ear the age old taboos of not upsetting other family members. But ask yourself this: did the family member in question ever feel guilty about the demands they constantly made on you, or the distress and anxiety they continued to pile on to you over the years? Somehow I don't think so.

If you really do have to keep in contact them then use the **distraction** technique. As soon as they start to moan or bombard you with their negativity, **change the subject** and distract their attention onto something positive. It can take a few attempts, but it's worth persevering. Very often once these brain drainers realise that they can no longer impose themselves and their problems on to you, they will begin to look for other victims.

Brain Drainers are also not noted for their sensitivity. Besides, any lingering feelings of guilt at keeping them at arms' length will be far outweighed by the **sense of relief in freeing yourself** from their oppressive company. Feelings of guilt are simply feelings after all, and as with any feelings they can be changed as soon as you decide to change your thoughts about them. It's really a question of survival, your own survival. In order to free yourself and begin to really **Walk on the Grass,** you must first cut away any dead wood that may still be clinging to you, holding you back, dragging you down, distilling your energy and your moods and making it impossible to move towards a different and better future.

> *And now at this point, I'd like to ask you a question: If you knew for certain that there would be no unpleasant repercussions and that you would feel no guilt in distancing yourself from Brain Drainers, would you still have the same friends, and the same relationships with family members as you do now?*

If the answer is yes, then you either need to work with them to improve your relationship or perhaps you are not yet willing to examine your relationships as closely as you might. If the answer is no, then it's time to move on.

CHALLENGE THEIR NEGATIVE THINKING

Distancing yourself from friends and family relations will never be an easy step to make, and should only be undertaken as a **final resort** after every effort has been made to maintain any relationship that can still provide mutual benefit. In the case of borderline Brain Drainers, it may be possible to **transform** their negative influence on you into a much more positive one by **challenging them**, **distracting them** and **encouraging them** to get involved with some of the exercises we looked at in previous chapters:

> ❋ *Build a Bonfire*
> ❋ *Encourage them to change their phone names*
> ❋ *The 20/80 Solution*
> ❋ *The Pendulum of Choice*

If, after undertaking some of these activities, you see no signs of change in your 'brain drain' friend or family member, then you need to be aware that you may be dealing with a **'Sabotaging the Crops'** scenario, and that your 'friend' is inwardly convinced that he or she has a valid reason for remaining negative and unhappy.

Unfortunately, there are those people who appear to want to make misery a full-time career, usually because the habit of complaining about everything has become so established in them that to remove it would leave a vacuum that either they are not capable of, or they could not be bothered to fill. If this is the case, then it really is time that you **put some distance between you**. Remember, you cannot be held responsible for how other people feel. When you have given as much consideration as you can to them, it's time to ask yourself what exactly are they giving back to you?

There is absolutely no point to maintaining a friendship simply out of sympathy or because you're afraid of the repercussions of ending that friendship. Once you realise that that there is nothing to be gained from continuing to pursue a lost cause, you will **stop wasting time** and energy and begin to put it to a much more rewarding use. And if you're still feeling charitable, remember that there are much worthier causes to which you could devote your efforts.

FORGIVENESS

Moving on from the past can be extremely difficult, especially after you have been deeply hurt by someone, perhaps friends or family. This is because we are unable to move on without first giving **forgiveness**, one of the most powerful of the emotions, but possibly the most difficult to express. In fact the inability to forgive is probably the greatest single factor to keeping us firmly trapped in the past. If you are unable to genuinely offer forgiveness, you are likely to conform to one of the following two states of mind:

- ✳ Maintain a constant aggressive state in which you try to get even with another person for what you imagine they have done to you, or;
- ✳ Obsess about your situation to the exclusion of all else, complaining to anyone and everyone who will listen about the

wrong you felt has been done to you. As a result not only will you be carrying the weight of your own negative thoughts, but you will be carrying the image of the person you wish to move away from constantly in your mind.

Don't underestimate the damaging and demoralising effect of carrying negative thoughts of this magnitude. To give you some idea of the **energy required** to maintain either of these states, just imagine having a huge rock permanently strapped on to your back, something so heavy that your back feels as though it will break and your legs buckle beneath you with each faltering step you take. But for all this intense effort, there are two things you **cannot change** in circumstances like these, no matter how you may try: The **past** itself and the **other person** involved. So if you can do nothing about either, make a pact not to continue to carry that heavy weight around with you any longer. In fact, the only way you will ever get to finally put that rock down is **to give forgiveness to the party** who you believe has wronged you.

MOVING ON LETTER

One of the most effective ways I have found to achieve this desired closure with forgiveness, is as follows:

- ❋ **Write a letter** to the other person involved, explaining exactly what you feel they did to you.
- ❋ Write down all the **details** of how their actions have affected you.
- ❋ Write down what you **believe** you have lost or suffered through their actions.

🌿 If some things you may be feeling, as you write your letter, become difficult to express, attempt to **draw a picture** which might better represent the issue with the other person. Use whatever creative method you choose, but express yourself on paper as fully as you can.

🌿 Give a **detailed evaluation** of what you consider to be the financial cost of their actions. That's right; put a monetary value on the damage you feel they have caused you. If you genuinely feel the damage amounted to a million pounds, then include that amount in the letter. But, whatever figure you arrive at, make sure to put a monetary value on it.

🌿 Having made your evaluation, **realistically consider** the chances of that amount of money **ever being repaid** to you. Also anticipate that you will not receive any financial settlement, explaining in the letter that you know that they have no way of ever paying that outstanding debt they owe to you.

🌿 Explain that you are going to **write off the debt**, as you know they can never repay it.

🌿 Your final words to end the letter are: **I forgive you.**

Now comes the final and most difficult part of the act of forgiveness. **Do not send the letter** to the person concerned because this would maintain the connection between you, and you may get a response which will continue the relationship, possibly in an even more negative way. What you really need to do now **is to let go,** to let go of the past and to let go of the person who has wounded you so deeply.

In order to do this, you must now decide how you will **dispose** of your letter because only by disposing of it are you really letting go of the hold this has on you. Perhaps you could burn it on a bonfire, tear it up or even bury it. It really doesn't matter what method of destruction you choose for the letter, but I recommend that you don't hold on to it for too long. Because only when you have finally destroyed the letter can you consign your sadness, anger and disappointment to the past, and **release yourself from the hold** the other person had over you. You need to finally let go and move on with your life.

ARE YOU A CUP OR A SPONGE

Pete was only 10 years old, and had just been selected to play football for a local team. A very sensitive boy, he was finding it difficult to take the very vocal criticism of the other boys whenever he made a mistake on the field. Often the cruel words they yelled at him would reduce him to tears. Pete didn't **understand** that their comments weren't intended to be hurtful or personal in any way; it was simply their raucous, boyish way of expressing their passion to win the game.

Then the day came when Pete became so upset at the prospect of this continual criticism, that he confided in me that he really didn't want to play any more. Tears were in his eyes, and he was very distressed. The game was due to start again, and I knew I would have to **act very quickly** if I was to attempt to change Pete's mind. I was acting as a volunteer first-aider that day, and was carrying a bucket of cold water. Immediately, I directed Pete to look at the bucket of water. In the bucket were a **cup and a sponge**, which I used as a revival aid for any boy receiving knocks during the game.

"**Imagine**," I said to Pete, "That bucket of water represents all the nasty, negative words you are likely to hear from the other boys during the game. And now," I said tipping some of the water onto the sponge, "imagine that when we pour the water on the sponge, the **sponge absorbs** all the nasty, negative words and locks them into the fibres of the sponge. Now," I continued, asking Pete to hold the cup and tip it upside down. "When we pour water over the **cup**, notice how the **water immediately runs off**. You see, cups don't absorb nastiness or negativity, Pete. They just let the water run off them. And even if you turn the cup the right way up and it catches the water inside, the water can still be thrown away very easily." Pete looked at the water trickling out of the now empty cup. "So, Pete," I asked him, **"do you want to be a cup or a sponge today?"** Pete's eyes lit up as he appeared to grasp the meaning: "I'm a cup, I'm a cup!" He said brightly. Pete went back on to the field and played his best football game ever.

You too can choose to be either a cup or a sponge, when it comes to reacting to cruel or negative words, thoughts or ideas from other people. You can either absorb and retain them, ensuring they continue to hurt you and cause you constant pain, or you can let them simply **bounce off you**, trickling away like water off the back of a cup. Once you decide that you are not going to allow other people to continue to hurt or upset you, they will be unable to do so.

THE GARDEN SHED IS NOW FULL

In this final chapter we've examined the imperative of looking after the **most important person** in your life — YOU! And we've given reasons why you will never be able to add to the safety, security or happiness of anyone else, until you yourself are safe, secure and on the way to happiness.

- ❈ We've also looked at the empowerment of **forgiveness**, and how it can liberate us from distressing experiences of the past, and allow us to chop away the influence of those we also wish to leave behind us.
- ❈ You'll also now be fully aware of the advantages of acting as a **cup rather than a sponge**, so that you no longer need to keep absorbing the unpleasant and negative words, thoughts and ideas of other people.

Well done, you now have a full set of tools in your garden shed;

- 🌿 A **garden axe** to cut out the weeds that strangle your well being to allow you to leave the Brain Drain Team behind and focus on your Success Team.
- 🌿 A **watering can** to nurture those much loved goals that need careful care and attention.
- 🌿 A **garden knife** to cut out the excuses you tell yourself why you have to dress as you do and start dressing like you have the confidence of the nation behind you.
- 🌿 A **pair of shears** to trim down those negative thoughts and replace them with some healthy productive thoughts.
- 🌿 A **garden hand trowel** to dig out those seeding events that have swayed your beliefs and plant some new seeds for the future
- 🌿 A **pair of pruning shears** to cut away the dead wood and re-engage with real fun and enjoyable childhood activities.
- 🌿 A **hand fork** to rake up that healthy soil from under the surface and be the best decision maker you've ever been, taking a logical healthy approach to risk and reality

EPILOGUE

Your particular journey is just building momentum now, and I sincerely hope that you have found the paths we have walked along interesting and instructive. Above all, this book has really been about how the choices you make define the life that you will lead. So please continue to make your choices the best that you can possibly make:

Choose your own preferred company, your own relationships; surround yourself with people who add to the enjoyment of your life, and distance yourself from those who detract from it, bringing only disadvantages and few if any benefits; learn to be content in your own company, and within the company you choose to keep.

As far as possible, surround yourself with creative people, and allow your own creativity to flourish in order that you may achieve greater personal success than you could ever have imagined possible.

Look to establish the real and authentic you, and be the best that you possibly can be. Learn how to forgive so that you can free yourself from the disappointing experiences and people of the past.

If you can begin to do all these things, then you really will know what it feels like to walk on the grass.

WALK ON THE GRASS

USEFUL INFORMATION

NEWSLETTER

Sign up for my newsletter at www.angelawhitlock.com and gain some valuable help in keeping the garden of your mind nourished.

The author's website
www.angelawhitlock.com

CDS & MP3 DOWNLOADS

Hypnotherapy CDs available from www.angelawhitlock.com

WORKSHOPS AND SEMINARS

Walk on the Grass Workshops run regularly, please check the website for a full programme of events at www.angelawhitlock.com

RECOMMENDED READING

Paul McKenna, *Change Your Life in Seven Days,* Bantam Press 2004
Windy Dryden, *10 Steps to Positive Living,* Sheldon Press 1994
Daniel Goleman, *Emotional Intelligence*, Bloomsbury Publishing 1994
Abraham Maslow, *Motivation and Personality*, RR Donnelley & Sons 1971
Michael Neil, *Feel Happy Now*, Hay House Publishers 2007
Karol Jackowski, *Ten Fun Things to Do Before You Die*, Hyperion 2000
Paulo Coelho, *The Alchemist*, Harper Collins 1999